ESSENCE OF SENSES

ALSO, BY SANTIAGO DIZON

WHEN BOYS BECOME MEN

DRUMS RUM-TUMMING

ESSENCE OF SENSES

A Book of Poems - Revised Edition

Santiago Dizon

Copyright © 2022 by Santiago Dizon.

Library of Congress Control Number:	2022921845
ISBN: Hardcover	978-1-6698-5702-0
Softcover	978-1-6698-5701-3
eBook	978-1-6698-5703-7

All rights reserved. No part of this book may be reproduced or transmitted in any form or by any means, electronic or mechanical, including photocopying, recording, or by any information storage and retrieval system, without permission in writing from the copyright owner.

Any people depicted in stock imagery provided by Getty Images are models, and such images are being used for illustrative purposes only.
Certain stock imagery © Getty Images.

Print information available on the last page.

Rev. date: 12/07/2022

To order additional copies of this book, contact:
Xlibris
844-714-8691
www.Xlibris.com
Orders@Xlibris.com
848654

For my pals Richard Reinbolt and Steve Soto. And all the silly folk out there...

ACKNOWLEDGEMENTS

· · · · · · · · ·

Meet Joanne Keliher, the 'Girl Next Door'. Jo helped me fix problems, whenever I pushed the wrong button on this machine, and everything went KABLOOEY! "Keep calm. Coach", and sure enough, Jo had everything a GO again. Don't tell her, but I pretended difficulties, now and again. Joanne is also good for my reputation.
Thank you, Toots.

PRAISE FOR WITH ESSENCE OF SENSES…by Santiago Dizon

"There's a couple of good ones,
if you read far enough."
Sister

"I kinda liked the one about the fan dancer."
Jim Dyson

"Roses aren't always red."
Anonymous

"Poetry is my favorite genre. Can anyone
recommend a good poetry book?"
Jane Claus

"Santiago cannot find a word to
rhyme with orange or purple."
The Committee for Fair Quotes

"Don't forget discombobulate."
Committee for the Confused and Disconcerted

"I remember Santiago and his best
pal, Bill Hushaw, in school. They were
both mainly discombobulated."
Principal McMasters

PRAISE FOR WHEN BOYS BECOME MEN by Santiago Dizon

"Gotta read it one of these days."
Sister

"At least this project kept him out of the bars for a while."
Gary Schwab

"I remember when Santiago got in a fight with Dick Christianson right in the middle of the crosswalk at Hoover High School. Dick said there was no Santa Claus and Santiago slugged 'em. Sorry, what was the question again?"
Principal Mr. McMasters

"Nice little book to take along when camping. Don't forget the matches."
Johnny Lopez

"I knew he deserved that 'C' grade I gave him in English."
Mrs. Judy Davis

"Santiago was so proud to have graduated in the top eighty-fifth of his class. When Men Become Boys proves he deserved his ranking."
Classmate

PRAISE FOR DRUMS RUM-TUMMING by Santiago Dizon

"I warned him, but he never listens to me."
Sister

"Ya gotta admit, he's got nerve."
Eddie Edgecomb, classmate

"My advice is to drink some rum with *DRUMS RUM-TUMMING.*"
Julie Miranda, critic

"My advice is to take some Tums for *DRUMS RUM-TUMMING.*"
Jeanne Adler, second-grade teacher

"I live in Alaska where it's very, very cold and sometimes it is hard to sleep. *DRUMS RUM-TUMMING* makes me drowsy every time I start it."
Cindi Walker, salmon fisher

"At least it has a pretty cover."
Georgia Bocchini Hellmers, chef di cunina

"Just happened to find *DRUMS RUM-TUMMING* on a bench at the bus station, traded it for a pack of gum."
Neville Hansen, entrepreneur

"I thought *RUM TUM-TUMMING* was
the sound from a drum."
Denis Biggs, producer

"*RUM TUM-TUMMING* is like reading
a game of musical chairs."
Mike Pithey, golfer

"Santiago is the ostrich of bird walkers."
Jimmy James, thinking man

CONTENTS

- - - - - - - - -

Poetry 1
Syllabary 2
Versivication 3
Essence of Senses 4
Remove Hi from History and Waddaya Got? 5
The Ballad of Robin Houde 7
Hennessey 9
Paul Bunyan and Babe, the Blue Ox 11
Off to See the Elephant 13
Mountain Men 15
Wagons Ho! 18
Hin-Mah-Too-Yah-Lat-Kekt Thunder Rolling Down The Mountain 19
Bonanza 21
California's First Tweet 23
Hell's Half Acre 25
Eureka 27
The Old Timer 29
Knights of the Road 31
Romance of the Ranchos 33
Blizzard of OZ 35
Let's Pretend 37
The Ant and the Grasshopper 39
Go for Broke 40
Tippecanoe and Tecumseh Too 43
Uncle Remus 46
Fee-Fi-Fo-Fum 49

Happy Valentine's Day 51
Paul Bunyan and Babe, the Blue Ox...52
Open Sesame 54
The Count of Monte Cristo..56
The Adventures of Tom Sawyer 59
To Have or Have Not...62
Jungle Book...63
Tortoise and the Hare..66
Pachyderm Pup 68
Toys Will Be Boys 71
Icarus 74
An Unexpected Journey 77
Jim Smiley and His Jumping Frog* 81
Animal Farm..83
Bonnie & Clyde 86
Carnivorious Vulgaris and Accelleratii Incredibus 87
The Little Red Hen 89
The Taxman..91
A Palatte..93
City Ditties 95
Obtuse 'Histerical' Verse 100
Munchies 105
Homo Neanderthalis...106
Goldilocks...107
Nude Dude 109
Ransom of Red Chief..110
Little Red Riding Hood 112
Elementary, My Dear Watson 114
Monster Mash..116
Sweet Carolyn 118
Greatest Generation 120
Say It Ain't So, Joe...122
Bully 124
Fued Fools..126
Bay State 127

Little Green Men	128
Over the Rainbow	129
Have Gun----Will Travel	132
The General	135
Satchel the Saige	137
Da Biscuit	139
Bright Path	142
Buccanneers	144
Bonnie & Clyde	146
'Another Fine Mess '	147
'Get Your Kicks '	149
Il Milione	151
Fair Dinkum	153
Run Bear, Run	155
Johnny	157
More Stoopid Stuff	158
If You Thought that was Stoopid, Just Wait!	163
Ogden Gnash Wanabees	166
Yes, It is Green Cheese	171
The Better Half	173
Yeahhhhhhh Buddy	174
Gotta Know the Territory	176
Returning from Shiloh	180
Mary	182
Signs of the Times	183

POETRY

* * * * * * * * *

Literature that evokes a concentrated imaginative awareness of experience or a specific emotional response through language chosen and arranged for its meaning, sound, and rhythm.

The rose is red
The violet's blue,
Let's have a go
And see if it's true.

SYLLABARY

Only twenty-six letters can be used
With millions of writings to yet be perused,
Think of the future when more will be read
Some with delight, others with dread.

Without a vocabulary with which to think
Ideas can't be offered in pencil or ink,
Language is precious for rhyme and for prose
Vital to read so one's mind doesn't close.

Novels or poems or scripts, even choral
Intensive, extensive, or silent or oral,
Conveying some notions that might feed the soul
Could find its way to treatise or scroll.

Speeches and lectures, conversations abound
If you can't understand, there's no common ground,
Might help someday, maybe strengthen a stance
So, thank all your mentors whenever you chance.

VERSIVICATION

. . . .

Poetry is more than making words rhyme
Themes should be clear, at least part of the time,
Some are composed with a camouflaged message
Somewhere is found a faint trace of vestige.

Verses oft scrambled and not over easy
Don't try so hard, might make you less queasy,
Bards treat words as codes and as symbols
Can breaks one's brain, like a symphony's cymbals.

The approach to a poem is most often a theme
And for the authors, they may have a scheme,
Lyric pieces might elicit strong feeling
While narrative poems are sometimes appealing.

An ode or a sonnet or an epic or ballad
Might make postulation and hypothesis valid,
Iambic pentameter needs five metric feet
To solve this mystery would seem quite a feat.

Then there's Haiku and limericks...

ESSENCE OF SENSES
. . . .

Blossoms drift from yonder trees
And clouds pass by as wannabees,
Visage appears, if look with soul
Often changing to faces of troll.

A stream nearby with tranquil laugh
Transports life amidst the chaff,
Clean and cool, for now at least
Changing course from west to east.

Time slips by and always will
Treasure moments till life is still,
Seek your chance and even more
Dance the dance, then leave the shore.

REMOVE HI FROM HISTORY AND WADDAYA GOT?

....

Our story begins with the first written word
Before that time, it's all kinda blurred.

Archeologist's dig and sometimes find
What Australopithecus had on his mind.

Civilization yawned in that vast Fertile Crescent
Before the tillage, it was mostly quiescent.

Both Euphrates and Tigris gently glide
Where the first Sumerians decide to reside.

Cuneiform evolves the first written word
With the invention of writing, ideas will be spurred.

Mesopotamians raised cities, with specialized labor
Now there were folks, one could call on as neighbor.

Assyrians were noted for their wild, warrior fashion
Would put plenty folks under, without a compassion.

Hammurabi then ruled and his Gardens were hung
Where shrubs, and vines, and flowerpots swung.

Across that page on a library's atlas
Advancement on Nile, comparably matchless.

Their story's exposed on those papers' papyrus
Expressing their tales of Set and Osiris.

Scientists dig, find mummies wrapped
In fine linen bandages, tightly strapped.

In the Valley of Kings, artifacts abound
Antique treasures placed under the ground.

Indus is the valley that hosts Pakistan
The area that later, Alexander overran.

Harappa and Daro, the oldest towns
So little is known, like who wore the crowns?

Dragon images in old Cathy
With dinosaur fossils, there's fears to allay.

Superstition's universal where science is truant
That's why humankind must be so pursuant.

Four-thousand year's history for the Chinese scholar
From emperor's silk to poor coolie squalor.

These narratives hint of a civilized life
How far have we come, through this rife and this strife?

THE BALLAD OF ROBIN HOUDE
· · · · · · · · · ·

In daes of olde when sume myn were bolde
There's a tale to shayre, which will now unfolde,
England's unsettled, King Richard's away
Fiteing the Saracens in the colde light of dae.

Lord Robin of Locksley, Saxon peasant defender
Enemy of Prince John, Norman regency pretender,
Sir Guy of Gisbourne, with the blessings of John
Taxed Saxon serfs from hither to yone.

Declared an outlaw by the sheriff and Guy
Sherwood Forest's a hideout, from there to defy,
A band of exiles, the fine Merry Myn
Will Scarlett, Friar Tuck, a noble thief's den.

Bandits they becume, robbing only Norman wealthe
Surprising rich caravans, using long practiced stealthe,
And the boote they gather is spread to the poore
Back at Nottingham they remain rotten to the core.

Maid Marion, a Norman ward, is secretly informing
At the same time to Robin, she's romantically warming,
An archery contest at Nottingham castle
All subjects invited, not only the vassal.

To arrest the bandit is the festival's intent
And Robin's an expert and wins the event,

He's discovered and captured, right into the slammer
But the desperado escapes, with the aid of some glamour.

Now, real history can spoil a really goode story
Richard never returns to reclaim his past glory,
He loses his life, while returning from battle
Never recouping his throne, or even his chattel.

Robin Houde had invented the Socialist party
Taking from the rich to give to less hearty,
Today he woulde practice as proude politician
While at the same time, remaining patrician.

HENNESSEY
. . . .

Listen my children and you shall learn
But ne'er a diploma shall you earn,
About that night in Sixty-Five
Hardly a man is now alive.

Hennessey, the bandit, was running quite late
After having his way with Big-Nose Kate,
He had laid his plans to steal the jewels
From the squire of land who followed no rules.

Two lanterns shone from the old castle's keep
Which shed some light for him to creep,
Over the wall with the aid of a vine
It was all accomplished, just before nine.

Through the Great Hall by slight candlelight
Tapers were glimmering, kept out the pure night,
Into the boudoirs where valuables hide
Hennessey found the gemstones abide.

If the constables followed by road or by lane
The outlaw had methods to deal out some pain,
Candles were lit in the taverns at night
Aids for their hero to help in his flight.

Two tapers dim meant the cops were nigh to
One taper bright meant the cops had no clue,

Riding his steed by village and farm
Soon placed Hennessey away from the harm.

The damsel's distress was her lover's astray
After selling the baubles, gave money away,
Big-Nose Kate in a mean, jealous rage
Put poor Hennessey straight in a cage.

The crowd was threatening in the old village square
Violence was imminent with only a dare,
Up on the gallows brave Hennessey swung
And that's why ballads of heroes are sung.

PAUL BUNYAN AND BABE, THE BLUE OX

. . . .

The geese flew backwards, and the fishes went south
  Even the hardiest were down in the mouth,
    Except for Paul who was out on a lark
      Hikin' the snowfields, always his park.

    Words froze solid before they were heard
    And all the noises were silently blurred,
    The white was dazzlin' and hurt the eyes
    The only sounds were brisk, breezy sighs.

    Paul on a jaunt in the woods this day
    Alone again, never needin' no sleigh,
    Alert to a bleat in the knee-deep snow
    Senses alert, in the cold, mornin' glow.

    And there a baby ox, as blue as blue
    You can look this up, everthin's true,
    A bran' new babe just hoppin' along
Spunky lil' critter and clearly quite strong.

    Takin' 'em home and warmin' 'em up
Could tell from the start, gonna be a good pup,
    Watchin' 'em grow, right from the start
      Got really big, right off the chart.

Forty-two axe handles twixt his eyes
Add a plug of tabacy, he grew to that size,
Et a ton a grain, and that's for lunch
'Jacks' in camp could heard the big crunch.

This yarn's about Bunyan and his partner, Blue
Betcha this story, ya' awready knew,
Some good ol' boys in those cold backwoods
Around a fire, can deliver the goods.

If you're ever in Minnesota on a holiday quest
Drive up north, 'stead of turning out west,
Most of these fellers know a story or two
And they'll always get better, if you buy 'em a brew!

OFF TO SEE THE ELEPHANT
. . . .

Third President Jefferson had dreamed an ambition
For American glory he needed a mission,
Captain Lewis's orders were heretofore stated:
Explore that Missouri, two years unabated.

Chosen to share in this great venture West
Clark's much more than merely a guest,
With command as a captain and a maker of maps
No discovery of theirs would fall into lapse.

Then Mandan was reached by boat and piroque
Forty men wintered, with the original folk,
Toussaint Charbonneau, such little to merit
But because of his wife, they were willing to dare it.

Teenaged Sacagawea was Charbonneau's mate
Helped the Corps in fulfilling their fate,
Her yonder Shoshone would achieve their needs
Befriending The People and buying their steeds.

Along the way, she gave birth to a son
And 'Pomp' will fill chapters, before he is done,
Baptiste will be found along the frontier
Steeped in yarn, mountain man premier.

Great Falls of the Missouri they portaged four-week
The explorers suffered hard, and their exploits were bleak,

Finally, the 'Divide' and Shoshone were found
Bird Woman returning with greeting unbound.

With Clark's slave, York, and Seaman the dog
They crossed those Rockies by river and log,
Through the high passes and into the dales
'Moccersins' ruined by cactus and shales.

Canoe the Columbia, all the way to the sea
Then finding way home was no guarantee,
A winter at Clatsop eating salmon Chinook
Corps waiting for spring and some elk meat to cook.

March 23rd, eighteen hundred aught six
They left for home and out of their fix,
Befriended again by Shoshone and Perce,
No man would complain or utter a curse.

Near the Three Forks, the captains would split
Exploring and charting the rivers with grit,
Meeting at the Yellowstone, they continued downstream
Into St. Louis, they completed their dream.

Stephen E. Ambrose said it the best
With Undaunted Courage they discovered the West,
Sometime reflecting if they saw it all now
Many discoveries under highway and plow.

From sea to shining sea, our nation has grown
Without exploration might never been known,
Because of this charge, some scholars have pondered
What might have happened if no one had wandered?

MOUNTAIN MEN
. . . .

(1810-1880)

Lewis and Clark opened the way
A path for a man to become émigré,
All kinds of men went to the peaks
To find the tracks to rich beaver creeks.

In the Eighteen Hundred's, sovereign men ventured west
Libertarian by nature they sought daring quest,
They had something special, that most men lack
Left home with a horse and a haversack.

The Platte was the river road that led the way
"Keep the flow in sight, and you can't go astray,
Be on the lookout for those wild Pawnee
Stay alert now, there's no guarantee".

Slowly, the Shining Mountains would come into sight
Hazy at first then a massive delight,
Now, climb those hills, find cold beaver streams
Then put your head down, you've earned your dreams.

The fashion in Europe was the beaver fur hat
But they had to find pelts in their own habitat,
Trapping in water up to their knees
After a while, would a breeze bring a freeze?

The Rocky Mountain Trapper opened emigrant trails
Around the campfires, there must have been tales,
Of Indians battles with the dreaded Blackfoot
And how they escaped after being ambushed.

Some Native Americans were cordial,
and some were hostile
None at that time could be truly called docile,
As a group, the Mountain Man followed no law
Some stayed celibate, most took a squaw.*

The 'Company' hired many and some trapped free
And most of their furs went over the sea,
At season's end, they met rendezvous
Drank barrels of whiskey and ate barbeque.

Jim Beckwourth, a Black man, was born into slavery
War chief of the Crow and famed for his bravery,
Kit Carson's the trapper who led expedition
That ushered in California's admission.

Jim Bridger built his fort, in the south of Wyoming
Ended his days of constantly roaming,
Colter, Fitzpatrick, both brother's Bent
With all those hardships, a life of content.

Jedediah Smith, first to overland Pacific
Struggled in the desert with adventures horrific,
Reaching California, feds slammed him in jail
Through trials and trails, Jed would prevail.

As with most of the fancies, few things endure
Ideas come along and change the allure,
Beaver in Europe fell out of the fashion
Silk prevailed and became the great passion.

DeVoto and Ambrose are the authors to read
If you want to proceed, to learn and succeed,
Take the hi out of history and wadaya got?
A story to recall right on the spot.

*My apologies

WAGONS HO!
. . . .

The Corps of Discovery opened the way
Which presented a challenge for the young émigré,
Trappers and traders were first to explore
Sought new beaver, like never before.

The wayfarer's mantra was 'Oregon or Bust'
Most of these pilgrims had lives to adjust,
Two thousand miles of a wagon trace
Twelve miles a day at a walking pace.

Up at four, with three hours of chores
A life of hardships in the Great Outdoors,
Johnnycakes prepared as the morning fare
Then there were harness and wheels to repair.

From Independence to the Willamette Valley
Missouri to Oregon with a deserving finale,
Half million, at the end, had traversed this trail
Then the Continental Railroad replaced it with rail.

Paiute and Sioux, Shoshone, and Ute
After some time, they were all destitute
Kiowa and Crow, and the Arapaho,
Along with the tribes, the buffalo.

HIN-MAH-TOO-YAH-LAT-KEKT
THUNDER ROLLING DOWN
THE MOUNTAIN

....

The Nez Perce befriended the Corps of Discovery
With trading, they aided the explorers' recovery.

Weary from the trials they faced on the trail
Aid from the Indians would help them prevail.

After that encounter, the die had been cast
It was inevitable, from the beginning,
that the peace could not last.

Fertile land for farming, then the discovery of gold
The Wallowa Valley was a sight to behold.

Then settlers arrived and claimed their land
The original folk were simply outmanned.

Six million acres, the Feds took away
Left only a sixth, to the Nez Perce dismay.

Resisting reservation, some settlers killed
No chance for solution, White blood had been spilled.

With Chief Joseph guiding, these Americans escaped
No chance for a peace, their future's been shaped.

Seven hundred refugees fled two thousand Yanks
The Nez Perce' fought them, on all of the flanks.

Episode ended, after a three-month chase
This chapter is finished without a disgrace.

"From where the sun now stands, I
will fight no more forever"
History proclaims such a noble endeavor.

BONANZA

. . . .

The Mexican War's over, California's a prize
Vast wealth was concealed, camouflaged with disguise,
For deep in the Sierra sequestered in streams
A mineral was hiding, an answer to dreams.

James Marshall was first, to find the shiny metal
Many Argonauts followed, all testing their mettle,
From 'round the world, 'Forty-niners' invade
Some hit pay dirt, most others betrayed.

As a group they were determined to
at the least take a chance
And many who arrived had little finance,
Sourdoughs and romantics all joined the quest
Hopeful and determined, many obsessed.

Seekers came by land and from across the seas
Latin America and Europe and even Chinese,
Across desert and mountain, the California Trail
Or 'round the horn to find golden grail.

The American River's where all this began
With determination and hope, they searched with a pan,
Their quest was the chance to finally strike gold
Knee-deep in mountain river, running so cold.

Three hundred thousand émigré found their way west
From all walks they poured, seeking nuggets to wrest,

Teachers and farmers and merchants and more
Many were greenhorns, others hard-core.

Businessmen earned riches, never went to the streams
Gamblers and bandits also working their schemes,
Sam Clemens made a name while visiting the mines
The diggings were found, where the oaks met the pines.

Today, one can chance souvenirs of this tale
Highway forty-nine is the Mother Lode trail,
Colima, Angels Camp, and ol' Placerville
Is where this yarn opens, at renowned Sutter's Mill.

Then folks with a conscience studied the scene
Found many participants black-heartedly mean,
Will we learn from the wrongs that greedy men made?
History must be taught, so lessons don't fade.

CALIFORNIA'S FIRST TWEET
. . . .

Mail seemed essential to the Golden State
'Cause gold had been found in Forty-Eight,
Prospectors and businessmen needed the post
Correspondence to stretch from coast to coast.

Joining as a free state in Eighteen-Fifty
All accomplished, swiftly and nifty,
California's pay dirt's a welcome bonus
Problems remained with stagecoach slowness.

Mounted young horsemen began in Missouri
A successful enterprise with plenty of fury,
Gallop to Sacramento in ten days the goal
With riders and horses under control.

Forbidden to drink anything 'strong'
Even a cuss word was considered a wrong,
Faithful and honest, a requirement must
Only some water to 'cut the dust'.

Distance between stations, what broncos could dash
Aware of the dangers, they were young, they were brash,
Depots for chargers placed ten miles apart
At a fast gallop, what horses could dart.

There's danger lurking in those shadows up yonder
But riding too fast to wonder or ponder,
And that smoke in the sky wasn't there before

Better skirt that gully, than proceed and explore.

One fifteen-year-old youngster carried the mail
Over the plains, he followed that trail,
Riding the desert and through that dust
Buffalo Bill Cody was one you could trust.

The riders received one hundred in pay
While unskilled workers earned a dollar a day,
Riders weighed in at a hundred twenty-five
Through stressful strife, they would always arrive.

Experiment lasted just under two years
Carried the post to western pioneers,
Technology advanced the telegraph wire
Time for that romantic, Pony Express to retire.

HELL'S HALF ACRE

· · · · · · · · · ·

It was mostly a slum, a real shantytown
Hosting five hundred of little renown,
Twenty-five thousand shortly to grow
It's Eighteen Forty-Nine, and the
world would soon know.

The 'Coast' was birthed in these wild, western days
Violence and vice support shady malaise,
It all began with the shouted word, 'GOLD'!
The City's overwhelmed with the desperate and bold.

The 'Hounds' served as 'Regulators',
a gang which preyed
On Mexicans and businessmen, a soldier's charade,
Confronted by cabal, they cowardly fled
Frisco's turned feral and chilling to tread.

Criminal-politician is the mixture that's brewed
Boomtown's corrupted, rude and quite crude,
Greed's the engine, propels some to power
At the end of their story, they'll devour then sour.

The 'Ducks' were next to spread their crime
Thugs from 'Down Under', it's a race against time,
Vigilante justice takes over The City
Politics and graft, ever so gritty.

'The Coast' was the haunt of the low and the vile

Fermented energy to seduce and beguile,
Debauching dives and opium dens
Not exactly the scene for souls to cleanse.

Patrons were slipped surreptitious Mickey Finn
Awoke with hangovers and so much chagrin,
Shanghaied on a clipper ship way out to sea
Press-ganged sailor and abductee.

The earthquake clobbered this Barbary Coast
Shook the place from pillar to post,
Renaissance resulting gentrified and tame
And brought to the zone a new kind of fame.

The Eighteenth Amendment along with reform
Prohibition for a while, then a new kind of norm,
Replaced with jazz and transgendered folk
Is he a girl or is she a bloke?

EUREKA

California's the name for this mythical isle
Amazon warriors with gold to beguile.

Native Americans had discovered it first
Coast and hills and deserts interspersed.

Pre-Columbians for thousands of years
They walked from the North, as true pioneers.

Enter españoles, conquistadors and church
The padres found thousands of souls to search.

Junipero Serra founded the missions
The padres brought Indians such different traditions.

Twenty-one missions, a long walk they strode
El Camino Real, the king's own road.

Mexico ruled next, 'cause Spain was weak
Indians misused, the Spanish technique.

Ranchos with cattle on a thousand hills
Caballeros y vaqueros rode with their skills.

Marshall found gold, which triggered the 'Rush'
But few of the Argonauts ended up flush.

They sailed 'round the horn and blazed western trail
Thousands with hope and so much travail.

Nowadays, it seems a quite different place
Gotta hurry up, gotta increase your pace.

Up there on the hill, there's that Hollywood sign
And down in the city, fine places to dine.

San Francisco rewards with that beautiful span
Fun to drive over in a car or a van.

And in between there's hamlets galore
Some things to abhor, some things to adore.

'A sun-kissed miss said, Don't be late!
That's why I can hardly wait,
Open up that Golden Gate!
California here I come!'

Al Jolsen

THE OLD TIMER
. . . .

The day was shuttin' down when he rode into town
San Miguel was all dusty, all covered in brown,
All the fella needed was some beans and a bed
His hip was achin', for he carried some lead.

The Pecos Kid was wild in those long-ago days
So many towns in between, it was beginning to haze,
He had challenged that dude, that day in his past
The hombre was a pro, his draw really fast.

He had come out ahead in that showdown at noon
Outside on the street, outside the saloon,
They slapped leather together, one slightly tame
The expert was history, and the cowboy was lame.

He once was lightning, fast on the draw
So much so, he attracted the law,
Sheriffs and marshals all asked him to leave
Before someone else had someone to grieve.

A rep had been earned, even though it was spurned
He was slowing way down; he should be concerned.
Hopefully, those times were over and done
His mission is to search for his wife and his son.

Probing town's records, no family to find
Time to move on, maybe life was divined,
One beer for the road, in the town's only bar

And there he was the young man with the scar.

The Pecos Kid was fast but not fast enough
He thought the young fella was only a bluff,
Now, it's Scar's turn to carry that burden around
Until it's his time to be put under the ground.

The Old Timer was buried in the town's Boot Hill
The greenbacks he carried barely covered the bill,
The Kid's trail's forgotten, his story is dust
Along with his iron all gathering rust.

KNIGHTS OF THE ROAD
. . . .

A hobo ain't a tramp and a hobo ain't a bum
They ain't neither lazy and they ain't neither scum.

Between that Rebellion and the Second World War
The American story surely bred myth and lore.

In the Eighteen Sixties, this land was in flux
There's not much work, where men could earn bucks.

Tough times meant travel to search fickle work
Scarce jobs out yonder those men wouldn't shirk.

Degrees in those days didn't guarantee career
Without opportunity, many lives lived austere.

A hobo ain't a tramp and a hobo ain't a bum
Picking fruit a few weeks for a very small sum.

Transient labor mimicked that recurring dream
A dollar a day, like swimming upstream.

With options scarce and no safety net
Those men in the factories had no union to vet.

So, they did what they must, they rode the rails
Living out lives harder than nails.

Hobos seemed to have this cultish nobility
But camping in jungles brought local hostility.

The Depression helped foster this itinerant fate
Find a bit of work and catch the next freight.

A hobo ain't a tramp and a hobo ain't a bum
Some of 'em scholars, and some were alum.

ROMANCE OF THE RANCHOS

- - - - - - - - - -

Note: The following adventure is of one of the
storied histories of old California but is purely a
figment of the imagination of Johnston McCulley,
a native of Illinois, and the author who created this
man of vengeance, the Robin Hood of the West.
Serious scholars believe Johnston got his idea from
the bandito, Joaquin Murrieta. Rated PG 13 for
violence; no animals were injured in the unfolding
events, throughout this verse. PETA approved.

Talented horseman and swordsman
when returning from Spain
Finds residents of his pueblo treated less than humane,
Draconian changes he considers a crime
His respected father, the alcalde, has been forced to resign.

Corrupt Don Quintero's a villainous dictator
Commanding his pueblo as a miscreant traitor,
Ruling with the aid of the captain of guard
Diego's secret mission is to get him disbarred.

The old don is joyful with Diego's return
But extremely upset with his lack of concern,
The son has a plan that he must keep concealed
For the protection of his parents, he must build a shield.

Sophisticated and foppish and acting the dandy
Sporting some court tricks, with which he's quite handy,

But when the tapers are trimmed, and the lights go out
Masked avenger rides abroad, dispensing his clout.

Quintero has plans for his daughter, Lolita
And you can bet your boots, she's
an encantador señorita,
Lolita disapproves her most handsome suitor
He has much to offer, but he's acting so neuter.

Robbing from the rich who support foul regime
Zorro, the fox, develops his scheme,
One night he reveals himself, masked as the raider
She's knocked off her feet, by this charming crusader.

Leaving bold Z, wherever justice is served
Quintero's confused and becoming unnerved,
Apprehending bandito, number one concern
It's not that simple, he would soon learn.

Peasants and Indios find Zorro heroic
Inspired after decades of living so stoic,
En el oficina de guard, the reformer's revealed
No longer is persona a secret concealed.

In the resulting swordplay, the competition is glorious
They both are quite expert, but Diego's victorious,
The Pueblo of the Angels is again in safe hands
The Avenger and Lolita exchange wedding bands.

BLIZZARD OF OZ

. . . .

We all were happy when Dorothy returned
The problem was her bridges were burned,
Dorothy and Em are together again
And don't forget Toto and the little Red Hen.

But what about her friends she left behind?
Their bond was strong and quite intertwined,
There's never a day when the three don't lament
They try to be happy, but they're seldom content.

Scarecrow looked smart in his graduation gown
His straw was shiny, a very light brown,
Earning degrees in Science and Math
Maybe a career as an osteopath?

The wicked witch had melted away
If you remember, that was twelfth of last May,
The Cowardly Lion with his new-found pluck
Is no longer a bully or even a schmuck.

Now, the Tin Man was desperate because he had rusted
But with plenty of Pennzoil, he's been fully adjusted,
His new heart is pure, and it sounds real strong
Always looking for games of bridge or mahjong.

On the surface it seems they live fine lives
Everyone in Oz is giving high fives,
But their dreams at night are filled with fraught

Worrying about Dorothy, keeps them distraught.

The three agree it's time to venture
To get to Kansas and begin an adventure,
They applied at the consulate, receiving permission
After filling out forms, they were granted admission.

The Emerald City gave them a fitting adieu
The Munchkins sang, it was a big ballyhoo,
The Good Witch urged, during the pleasant episode
"You get there by following the Yellow Brick Road."

LET'S PRETEND

Humpty Dumpty's a most curious lad,
Rolly and polly, which wasn't the fad.

Christian Andersen's his Middle School,
Attending most often and playing the fool.

Humpty's classmate, Jack, was a real clumsy kid,
So often tripping, often landing with skid.

Not very nimble and not very quick,
Stumbled in the hall, over a candlestick.

Another companion, his name's Jack Horner,
A real boring kid, always sitting in corner.

Often heard bragging, "What a good boy am I",
Hump wanted to hit 'em, straight in the eye.

Ditching third period with a devious plan,
Peek at his favorite, freckled-faced Anne.

Sexes were separated by an orange, brick wall,
Had to be careful, not to slip and not fall.

Humpty climbed divider to gander at girls,
Beginning PE, sporting curls and their swirls.

A rumble at first, then a good, hard shake,
Wall is swaying, one really strong quake.

Sneak is slipping, he's lost his hold,
The chance he took for being so bold.

Cracking his head, on a playground swing
All because of a juvenile fling.

Humpty, as you know, resided in France,
That's the place of snails and romance.

All the king's men and all the king's horses,
Were out playing golf, on all those green courses.

THE ANT AND THE GRASSHOPPER

An allegory

The ant is industrious, working all summer long
He sweats while he labors, no time for mahjong,
Winter is coming and he must be prepared
Toiling all day, little time to be spared.

The grasshopper, on the other hand,
sings through the days
Scoffing at the ant with mocking clichés,
He's happily lighthearted, with an abundance of food
The ant's tireless work ethic cannot change his mood.

But the days grow shorter, and the land is stark
No leaves on the trees, no grass in the park,
It's rainy and cold, sometimes snow on the earth
While the ant's underground, cheerful with mirth.

The ant's in his basement, snug with his meals
Mr. Grasshopper's homeless, confused with ordeals,
Now, the ant has a conscience and shares his bounty
Suddenly, there are grasshoppers
from all over the county.

Hoppers form a union demanding their share
After all they reckon, it's only what's fair,
With the coming of spring, they're all 'ristocrats
They agreed in their caucus, they'd be Democrats.

GO FOR BROKE
. . . .

After school on Thursday with her homework complete
Mariko's playing tag near her Whittier Street,
The puppy, Tadashi, faithful and loyal
Watching his family and feeling quite royal.

Takeo's playing baseball, with his eight-grade pals
These stories taking place in western locals,
Moms, dads, the elderly, even the infirmed
Their very worst scenario has now been confirmed.

No prom for Midori nor graduation for Miki
Their lives will change, ever so quickly,
Suddenly the signs: NO JAPS ALLOWED
So many uncertain, under dark cloud.

Pearl Harbor's been attacked, our fleets destroyed
Coastal residents are quite paranoid,
Scenario plays out, early in the war
Homeland invasion fears, hard to ignore.

February of Forty-Two, history noted that date
Order 9066, with little debate,
On the Pacific coast, four vulnerable states
Japanese destined as federal inmates!

The president judged them a plausible threat
And isolating these people seemed a safe bet,
But the Constitution protects citizens, some aliens alike

In hindsight it seems to smack of Third Reich.

One hundred twenty thousand, more
than sixty percent citizens
Rounded up by the army and sent to these prisons,
Two-thirds were Nisei, and they were born free
Their citizenship status lacked a real guarantee.

Evacuees allowed only what they could tote
Including bedding and linens to places remote,
Tadashi and pets all left behind
No one knew where they might be consigned.

Lonely outposts, both hot and then cold
Uprooted Americans, new lives to unfold,
Tarpaper barracks and bathrooms exposed
A shocking reality for drastically deposed.

Uniformed army guards and barbwire fence
A dismal three years is now to commence,
With Japanese meijo they will soon earn esteem
Determination and will power to the extreme.

Eventually schools, even graduation dances
Along with the sports, took advantage of chances,
If willing to fight, young men offered an out
Patriotic Americans, there's so little doubt.

Fighting 442, most decorated in history
For these proud soldiers there was never a mystery,
Fourteen thousand served, ten thousand Purple Hearts

Unselfish heroism was way off the charts.

Go for Broke, their motto, for boys who became men
Hawaiian pidgin, again and again,
'We did our job it's as simple as that"
When back in the States, there's no welcome mat.

NO JAPS ALLOWED greeted them on their return
Few attitudes changed, they quickly will learn,
Twenty-one Medals of Honor and still no respect
They must get on with their lives and reconnect.

It was the social milieu of that time
'Yellow Peril' and xenophobia, a social crime,
Korematsu, in Forty-Four, challenged The Court
9066's upheld, with government's retort.

A half-century passes and finally redress
At last reparation helps heal that abscess,
E pluribus unum is a motto to cherish
If again we forget...a nation might perish.

TIPPECANOE AND TECUMSEH TOO

A comet streaked the skies, in eighteen eleven
Native Americans thought a sure sign from heaven,
Tecumseh's the leader of the Shawnee confederacy
His brother, The Prophet, a schemer accessory.

Away from Tippecanoe recruiting the Creek
Tecumseh was counting on this solar mystique,
William Henry Harrison's the military chief
Attacked his village, his soldiers the thief.

According to myth, Tecumseh fashioned a curse
That American presidents would find so perverse,
Eighteen Forty, Harrison's commander-in-Chief
Tecumseh, with locution, would cause him great grief!

"Harrison will die, before presidency's ended
With this curse, every generation extended,"
For the sake of argument, this means twenty years
Politicians, of course, would ignore all these fears.

Harrison served as leader for only twenty-eight days
Tecumseh said, "Gotcha", to paraphrase,
Expiring after speech, Harrison gave in the cold
The president's fate, dramatically foretold.

Eighteen Sixty, Lincoln's elected to office
He wasn't in the least, a bit overcautious,
Abe struggled two terms, with the stress of the day

After the Confederates had broken away.

Our American Cousin's presented that night
The Lincoln's expected an evening's delight,
President expired the very next morning
Did anyone remember Tecumseh's warning?

Fourteen months into Garfield's term
Shot by assassin, reports would confirm,
Eighteen Eighty, this deed took place
A nation was saddened, a need to replace.

Some might say that Harrison's to blame
Assault on Tippecanoe had brought him acclaim,
But the cost of this curse had a really high price
Three Heads of State, to be precise.

In Nineteen Hundred, it was McKinley's turn
This malediction should have been of concern,
Wounded shaking hands in cold Buffalo,
Anarchist's bullet dealt a deadly deathblow.

Vice President Roosevelt now takes command
Accepting leadership of this vast hinterland,
Served two terms, he coined 'Fair Deal'
And championed the Progressives and did it with zeal.

Watch out now, the story's getting scary
The curse should have made the presidents wary,
It's Nineteen and Twenty, and the die had been cast
And I'm sorry to report, he won't be the last.

Warren G. Harding was under that spell
Five that Tecumseh had said farewell,
In the next twenty years, was anyone nervous?
Did they think that jinx would ever again surface?

It's now Nineteen Forty, you do the math
Had the Native American erased his wrath?
FDR is the leader, through depression and war
The number of terms he was elected was four.

But Tecumseh's still around and part of the scene
His most terrible curse even more obscene,
Who will be next? I know you know
Come on, let's hear some braggadocio.

Nineteen Sixty, voting year of this tragedy
Getting real tired of that old Indian's strategy,
JFK's murdered, on a street in that Dallas
Shot by Oswald, who was callous with malice.

In Nineteen Eighty, a Republican's elected
Tecumseh was ready and had already selected,
One Whig, four Republicans, and two Democrats
No matter the party they were all bureaucrats.

The president this time would break 'The Curse'
Ronald Reagan, it proved, had no need of a hearse,
Shot in the chest during his term
The 40th survived...he had turned the worm.

UNCLE REMUS

Brer Fox's fed up with Brer Rabbit, a foe
That gosh-darn rascal's always adding to woe.

Scheming away, gonna trick that rabbit
He's tried so often, it's becoming a habbit.

Brer Fox sculps a tar baby, real-sticky, but cute
Gotta admit, it's an adorable coot.

Here comes Brer Rabbit, whistlin' the road
Fox hiding in bushes, quiet as toad.

Approaching strange creature, hare's doffing his cap
"A good morn to ya fella, you're a cute li'l chap".

Concealed in bushes, Fox's having his snicker
Turning out better than a sip of that liquor.

No answer of course, cuz the tar baby's mute
Answer ungreeted, "Don't you dare be a snoot."

Hidden by shrubbery, Brer Fox's tickled pink
Surely becoming the perfect hoodwink.

Again and again, Brer Rabbit insists
He's mad enough to start using his fists.

Over and over this scene plays out
Brer Rabbit has givin' his very last shout.

Brer Fox must be cautious to remain really quiet
As he aims to make that rabbit his diet.

Rabbit sticks and kicks at the stuck-up critter
He's all fed up and gettin' quite bitter.

Our heroes' extremities all attached to the glue
Brer Fox's real pleased, he's fastened in goo.

Brer Fox appears, Brer Rabbit's stuck fast
Finally, the victor's havin' a blast.

"I'll build a big fire, then I'll roast you and eat you
You'll taste real goodly, whenever I chew".

"Roast me! Hang me! Do as you please
But please, no briar patch, it's buzzing with bees."

"I'll toast you or hang you, but I have no string
Then I could watch you, enjoying your swing."

"Please Brer Fox don't throw me in patch
I couldn't survive such a scratchy ol' thatch!"

"The briar patch, eh? What a good idear
It'll shred you to pieces, you'll end up a smear."

Flinging that rabbit, right into that tangle
Into that stew, to mangle, then strangle.

Listening patiently, for that pitiful wail
Should be the end of this poor bunny's tale.

Quiet as braille, disappointed with hush
Expecting awful anguish coming back from the brush.

Brer Fox heard his name, from on up the road
A bit of a tease and a whole lotta goad.

"I was bred and born in that ol' briar wild"
And with that mock, Rabbit winked, then smiled.

FEE-FI-FO-FUM
. . . .

Young Jack farmed, with his widowed mum
Their plight was desperate and soon overcome,
Jack chopped and weeded, and milked their cow
Working all day, no money for plow.

Mum told Jack to sell Old Bess, and buy some seed
In the morning to the marketplace, it was agreed,
On the way to the market, met this funny old guy
Who proposed a deal, which might simplify.

"Trade me your milk cow, for these three magic beans
They grow overnight, it's all in their genes",
Jack showed his ma when he got home
She felt so bad, he wanted to roam.

Seeds out the window rather upset
Falling asleep with so much regret,
Waking at dawn, what do you think was spied?
A really big beanstalk, just outside.

Up the stem and into the cloud
"I must help my mother this time," he vowed,
The climb was rough, but well-worth the hassle.
Can you believe at the top, he found an ol' castle?

A citadel discovered right up in the sky
Maybe his chance to rectify,
Jack had some adventures with a giant and gold

One golden harp and a goose, I'm told.

To make a story short and I think it's time
It's becoming too hard to make a good rhyme,
Jack and his mother now rich and quite merry
Living happily after, which is customary.

HAPPY VALENTINE'S DAY

'Chi-Town' was lawless from Twenty to Thirty
Two gangsters ruled and the Tribune was wordy,
Town's divided 'tween Moran and Capone
Both need control of the mean streets alone.

Bootlegging had provided these hoodlums success
One of them soon, must be contented with less,
The north side of Chicago was Moran's refuge
And 2122 Clark Street would be his deluge.

Cleverly disguised as the constabulary blue
Scarface's crew were the hoodlums who knew,
Tommy guns erupted, and the site's all blood
Seven thugs slaughtered, face-down is the mud.

'Bugs' had escaped because he was tardy
His crooked empire never again to be hardy,
Capone took over and soon made a million
Not too bad for a Brooklyn civilian.

Then Eliot Ness was assigned to the fray
And after some time, put the gangster away,
Sentenced to 'The Rock', eleven years in the slammer
When released, the mobster was void any glamour.

PAUL BUNYAN AND BABE, THE BLUE OX

. . . .

The geese flew backwards, and the fishes went south
Even the hardiest were down in the mouth,
Except for Paul who was out on a lark
Hikin' the snowfields, always his park.

Words froze solid before they were heard
And all the noises were silently blurred,
The white was dazzlin' and hurt the eyes
The only sounds were brisk, breezy sighs.

Paul on a jaunt in the woods this day
Alone again, never needin' no sleigh,
Alert to a bleat in the knee-deep snow
Senses alert, in the cold, mornin' glow.

And there a baby ox, as blue as blue
You can look this up, everthin's true,
A bran' new babe just hoppin' along
Spunky lil' critter and clearly quite strong.

Takin' 'em home and warmin' 'em up
Could tell from the start, gonna be a good pup,
Watchin' 'em grow, right from the start
Got really big, right off the chart.

Forty-two axe handles twixt his eyes

Add a plug of tabacy, he grew to that size,
Et a ton a grain, and that's for lunch
'Jacks' in camp could heard the big crunch.

This yarn's about Bunyan and his partner, Blue
Betcha this story, ya' awready knew,
Some good ol' boys in those cold backwoods
Around a fire, can deliver the goods.

If you're ever in Minnesota on a holiday quest
Drive up north, instead of turning out west,
Most of these fellers know a story or two
And they'll always get better, if you buy 'em a brew!

OPEN SESAME
· · · · · · · · · ·

Wicked Hugalu Khan and his Mongol horde
Swept through Baghdad and vanquished with sword,
Caliph Hassan, betrayed the prince
A villain so rotten, should make reader wince.

Cassim, the scoundrel, both ugly and oily
The reason the Arabs invented the doily,
Ali, the son, and rightful heir
He's got what it takes, with plenty of flair.

Palace dejected, the good days have vanished
Our lionheart it seems, is totally banished,
Love is denied twixt Ali and Mara
Lovers must share a fond sayonara.

Escape to the desert, Ali wanders the wild
Never giving up hope to be reconciled,
Accidently, he finds a disguised, secret crypt
Outlaw treasure, he's sure that he's flipped!

Big Bandit Baba, Forty Thieves' big cheese
Adopts the lad, and lives as the breeze,
The caliphate's suffering, and Cassim's the cad
The prince cares less, he's more than just bad.

Ten years Ali rambles, harassing the Hun
Robbing from rulers and then on the run,
Overthrowing the Mongols dastardly rule

It'll takes some smarts, and Cassim is no fool.

Tyrant, Hugala affianced to Mara
Has a gift for the princess, a diamond tiara,
Then Ali is captured, it's death in the square
Baghdad is silent, steeped in despair.

Rescue by the thieves, and Mara as well
At the end of the day, everything's swell,
Revolution succeeds, there's streets of joy
Mostly because of a brave, bandit boy.

THE COUNT OF MONTE CRISTO

This is a tale, and it's not for the wimps
Follow along and have a close glimpse,
Edmond Dantes is our hero this time
A spiel about France and an odious crime.

After Napoleon's objectional trial
He's punished to Elba, a lifelong exile,
A lonely isle he's sent to lament
Less than a year till the 'Corporals' ascent.

Narratives rather muddled with jealousy and greed
Odious emotions where evil does breed,
Dumas paints drama swell in his tale,
Edmond is trapped and lies do not fail.

His friends have fashioned, insidious plot
Placing our hero in perilous spot,
Convicted of treason by friends who lie
Life in the slammer, where he's destined to die.

Damned to the island, a prison of doom
Surrounded by sea, a god-awful tomb,
Sadistic warden delights in the dread
Amused with the horrors, till all life has been fled.

Years have passed, Edmond's startled in cell
Where hopeless dreams desperately dwell,
Breaking through stone, surrounding his vault

A bearded, wild man, time to exalt!

Meet Abbe' Faria, ten years in this jail
Digging a tunnel, as slow as a snail,
They hollow a passage in a bid to be free
Scholarship and fencing taught, during this spree.

Seven years pass by to finish the job
Gifted a secret at mentor's last nod,
Map to an island, conceals Spada treasure
Enormous wealth of dazzling measure.

Replacing the body with himself in the shroud
Tossed off a cliff, Mediterranean cloud,
Freed from his cloak, he swims ashore
Encounters some pirates, time for valour.

A knife fight with raider, then sparing his rival
Aiding free Edmond with his total revival,
Working with pirates, then returning to France
In Marseilles he learns story, only by chance.

Jacopo, the pirate, and now loyal friend
Working together they create a good blend,
Sail to Cristo, discover vast wealth
Back to Paris, where they turn on the stealth.

The Count of Monte Cristo has planned a grand scheme
For years he's brooded, revenge is his dream,
Charming and clever, society's delight
Presenting himself as a blue-blooded knight.

The friends who perjured are all proven false
For these three cowards, it's the end of the waltz,
Femme fatale is next to explain
Her answer's complex and causes some pain.

Mercedes, his love, wed one of the three
She told the truth, it wasn't with glee,
Pregnant with Albert and Edmond's his dad
Because of no father, life would be sad.

Your task at hand is to complete this story
Possibly your finish is happy with glory,
But again, who knows? Perhaps it's quite tragic
What's of import is finding the magic.

THE ADVENTURES OF TOM SAWYER
....

Tom lives in the home of his strict Aunty Polly
And tattletale Sidney, little hint of a jolly,
Tom's being punished, played hooky from school
Polly doesn't want him ending up fool.

His penalty for transgression, must whitewash their fence
There's very little chance of him growing up dense,
Disappointed to forfeit this Saturday's rest
Persuades his friends to take away stress.

Swapping treasures for pleasures, to do all his labor
Kids seem pleased, to help out their neighbor,
Trades trinkets for tickets, wins Sunday School Bible
Bragging David and Goliath, two disciples, proved libel.

Pretty Becky Thatcher's the new girl in town
Affianced with Tom, but soon wears a frown,
'Cause he and Amy's been trothed before
She shows this romantic, two-timer the door!

Tom and Huck reconnoiter graveyard one night
Seeking cure for some warts, that might become plight,
Witness heinous murder by that spook, Injun Joe
Boys swear blood oath, running away adds to woe.

Town drunk Muff Potter, is blamed for this deed
Both lads agree it's time to secede,
Muff is arrested, and the boys suffer guilt

Feeling real badly, including the hilt.

The two scalawags, with Joe Harper, a chum
Escape to river-island and pretend pirate scum,
Petersburg believes the boys have all drowned
While on their retreat, merely running aground.

Sneaking home for their funeral, they're met with rejoice
Decision to return, they made the right choice,
Regaining Becky's favor, Tom nobly takes blame
Torn page in a textbook ignites the old flame.

Attending Muff's trail, Tom attests against Joe
What he has done is create vicious foe,
Villain escapes, court window's no hitch
Cutthroat considers Tom a big snitch.

Summer arrives, offers adventure a chance
In all that Mississippi River expanse,
Hunting for treasure in an ol' haunted home
Sun slowly setting with an eerily gloam.

Injun Joe's in the basement, with purloined gold
Scary experience for friends to behold,
Huck shadows scoundrel, Widow Douglas is saved
From evil blackguard, mentally depraved.

A bit later a picnic, in that warped Dougal Cave
Sweethearts are lost and try to stay brave,
With diminishing tapers, spy hideout of Joe
Tom must prove a most valiant beau.

Urgently searching, find twisted way out
Town then celebrates, not leaving a doubt,
The cave must be locked, Joe starving to death
Deserving wicked fate, he claimed his last breath.

Tom and Huck sneak back to the cave
Locate Joe's trove right close to his grave,
Stash is invested, but they couldn't care less
What capers are next is anyone's guess.

Widow adopts hero, karma and luck,
Civilized life is not for our Huck
He escapes confinement, wants back on the trails
Maybe some pirating, maybe riding some rails.

Tom promises Huck that if he returns
Could join his robber band, if that's what he yearns,
Huck agrees, and we must all chance a guess
What misadventures are next, for this naughty noblesse?

Twain set his novel in the Eighteen Forty's
Chronicles Tom and his chums, on some of their sorties,
Critique of society, with tongue in the cheek
Ironic hum with a bit of a tweak.

TO HAVE OR HAVE NOT

Jim and Della, most stressfully married
The times are hard and their feelings quite harried,
Especially at Yuletide, no money to spare
Sometimes they wonder, why life isn't fair.

Living together in a most modest flat
Their only extras, her gloves and his hat,
It's cold in their apartment with little to eat
Cheering each other is no easy feat.

They both must leave to seek a gift
Their minds, of course, all clouded with thrift,
Looking in windows, they don't have the means
They wish to be sharing much more than cold beans.

Della's proud pride is her long, lovely hair
The only thing extra that gives her some flair,
She decides to crop it and sell for gold chain
A most desperate resolve relieves her of strain.

Jim's only asset is a bequeathed gold watch
The only possession that lifts him a notch,
He sells his treasure to buy pricy comb
Expensive gift he's proud to bring home.

Opening their gifts on a cold, Christmas day
Underwhelmed at the most, they have little to say,
Finding themselves with naught to need
Love and sacrifice...the most-valued creed.

JUNGLE BOOK

Bagheera, the panther, roaming river one day
Evening's approaching, with a light touch of gray,
The forest is quiet except for the breeze
Alert as always, she's heard a faint sneeze.

Glued in the mud, a small boat in repose
Inside on a plank, a small boy in a doze,
What to do with this alien child?
Little creature discovered right there in the wild.

Introduces the man-child to wolf clan folk
After all, he's a cute little bloke,
Mowgli grows wild for another ten years
All forest animals becoming his peers.

Shere Khan's been spotted on nightly prowls
Hints of a man-child, spawns ghastly growls,
Bagheera volunteers to lead boy away
Or the lad could end up a tiger fillet.

The boy must be secreted out of harm's way
If he's to stay safe at the end of the day,
Man-village is the site that they must find
It's time for Mowgli to live with his kind.

The pair embark, as soon as it's dark
Their wilderness home, like living in park,
First night they sleep in a giant teak tree

But Kaa's quite near, hissing with glee.

Reptile is wily with spellbinding daze
Must be cautious of bewitching gaze,
Mowgli kicks python right off a bough
Eluding the serpent at least for the now.

The duo must separate, after a spat
Mowgli's been acting like a little spoiled brat,
Monkeys appear, take man-cub away
They want to do more than have fun and play.

Peril from Kaa in a primeval ruin
Then meeting Baloo, a slack, hippy bruin,
Bagheera reappears and the three consult
Man-village is answer, only way for result.

Then a committee of vultures, elect to adopt
But Khan arrives, the plans quickly dropped,
Baloo and Khan have a terrible brawl
Looks like the bear has given his all.

Mowgli ties a flame, to enraged tiger's tail
Khan's plan for murder is destined to fail,
Baloo recovers, and the three carry on
Their goal is to find a village by dawn.

Just when it seems, they've toiled hard and lost
They've given their all, no matter the cost,
Suddenly, a song drifts through the air
And look, by the stream, a damsel quite fair.

She pretends to be clumsy and spills water jug
Looking at pitcher, she gives shoulder shrug,
Mowgli to the rescue, he refills it for her
Then for some time, his life is a blur.

Howls through the jungle, the wolves are quite sad
Remembering their boy, truly missing their lad,
The stripling is learning new ways to adjust
Into new life, Mowgli's been thrust.

TORTOISE AND THE HARE
....

Once upon a time when creatures all spoke
One morning early after most had awoke,
Hare as usual was bragging his speed
Nothing 'specially odd for beasts of that breed.

He did little else 'cept eat grass and run
Rarely donating much wisdom or fun,
The glade was warming, the sky losing red
And here comes Tortoise, just out of his bed.

Hare always teased him for lumbering gait
Tortoise unhurried, rarely late for a date,
Hare was haughty ran circles galore
Never offering aid in a job or a chore.

Tortoise chipped in, whenever the chance
Completing a task, never needing to prance,
Tired of hearing Hare brag of his dash
Challenging that silly, might settle his hash.

The race was away, Hare quickly took point
Running in eights all over the joint,
Far in the lead, there's time for a nap
Here comes Tortoise, closing the gap.

Slow and steady reached finish line first
Day was closing, time to slacken his thirst,
Cheers from the forest awakened the Hare

Tortoise had won, honest and fair.

Hare had learned not to brag of his pace
Slow and steady had, after all, won the race,
In the passing years when men appear
The glade is still, there are humans to fear.

And that, amigos, is a story for next time.

PACHYDERM PUP

. . . .

The Great War was over, he's returning from France
Lost a leg in a battle, one can tell at a glance,
Back to the circus, looking for work
Holt is damaged, but no job will he shirk.

Assigned as caretaker of elephant folk
Welcoming job, he's got kids and he's broke,
Mrs. Jumbo's in the hay, birthing her calf
Holt's at her side, on her behalf.

Babe's unalike, sporting really big ears
Poles apart from the rest if his peers,
Camouflaged flaps, introduced to big show
Hard to keep secret, from patrons who'll know.

Pelting trash at performer is always, quite rude
And don't you forget, these creatures are nude,
Crowd erupts, pelting peanuts and more
Cleaning the joint's gonna be a big chore.

Dumbo, Dumbo, shouts from the crowd
Extremely rude, extraordinarily loud,
Mother, Mrs. Dumbo, goes into a funk
With a trumpet or three, right from her trunk.

Caused lotsa damage to main circus tent
Her love was loud, and she needed to vent,
Following the fracas, the mom's sold away
Only strategy to calm the big fray.

Joe and Milly, each one a young colt
These circus children belonging to Holt,
Consoling with Dumbo, he's lost his ma
Poor little guy, his feelings are raw.

By chance they find that Dumbo can fly
Just a start, of course, not high in the sky,
Encouraging friend with sympathy play
Back to the circus, there are bills yet to pay.

High on a platform, smoke, then a fire
Dumbo has a problem, situation is dire,
Flames and fear and riotous fright
Panic results, the crowd taking flight.

Dumbo finds water, flies over the throng,
Spraying the flames, his spuming quite strong,
Circus bought by Biggies, and moves to New York
Plenty of champagne and throw away cork.

In another risky skit, Dumbo's in danger
He trumpets in fear, in need of a ranger,
Mother's outside, hears calls from her boy
Like an all-out assault on the city of Troy.

Vile master has intentions to murder the dam
The good guys agree, 'bout time for a scram,
Escaping from greedy, villainous boss
If they stay lucky, it'll be owner's big loss.

Quickly to the harbor to find waiting ship
Elephants onboard to take the long trip,
Off to India, start living anew
No captive animals, furthermore, in the brew.

TOYS WILL BE BOYS

. . . .

When one hopes upon a star
Light which comes from far afar,
A desperate wish with faith and trust
One goes asleep with prayer a must.

Jiminy Cricket has found a home
Dry and warm with room to roam,
With Feline Fig and fish-Bowled Cleo
The three together, a fairy tale trio.

Geppetto carves a puppet, the image a lad
A lonely life has left him sad,
If blessed with a son, his life would be good
Might give him cause to shape his wood.

In the Land of Nod, where fancies come true
Granted by a fairy whose color is blue,
When Geppetto awakes his creation's alive
Bestowed with a gift, a son to thrive.

But the wish is partial, the boy's still pine
But much, much sweeter than Frankenstein,
Pinocchio must prove to be of merit
If it's a life that he'll inherit.

Without experience, the boy needs a guide
Jiminy Cricket to be allied,
A conscience is what the boy must search
If not remain made from birch.

"Give a little whistle, I'll come on the fly
Look for me, I'm your loyal ally,"
Cleo and Fig and Jiminy rest
All in the casa, so very blest.

Off to scuola, when the cricket's asleep
Dreaming delights and counting his sheep,
Sly fox, Foulfellow, and Gideon the cat
Conned the lad, the dirty rat!

Sold to the villain, Stromboli's his name
Bought marionette, hoping big fame,
A living puppet brings owner big riches
With lots of lira to stuff in his britches.

Stashed in a birdcage to guard his wonder
An escape's a disaster, a loss of his plunder,
Jiminy to the rescue, a whistle he heard
Pinocchio is there, cooped like a bird.

Blue fairy helps Jiminy set the boy free
Remember amicos, he's part of a tree,
To cover his faults, he tells some lies
His nose grows longer, a way to chastise.

A misadventure at Pleasure Park
Beer and cigars, but not quite a lark,
Boys changed to donkeys to work in the quarry
Luckily, Pinocchio has help from a fairy.

Meanwhile, his father is lost at sea
And perusing this tale, makes one weak in the knee,
Follow along, find what happens next
I for one, surely am vexed!

Escape at last, Pinocchio's home
Only to find that again he must roam,
Geppetto's boat is pitchpoled by gale,
Dad's swallowed whole, by Monstro, the whale.

Building big fire causes jumbo big sneeze,
All are expelled right with the breeze,
Geppetto is saved, but the puppet has perished
Woodcutter has lost the son he has cherished.

But don't despair, my readers and friends
We all are joyed, with true, happy ends,
The fairy grants life to the boy for his deed
Life happy after is just what we need.

Jiminy hops out the very next night
His Wishing Star is far, but bright,
Blue Fairy appears with a badge of gold
And this is the yarn that's mostly told.

ICARUS

Those ol' Greeks could be grim with their histories
When lessons were taught, explaining their mysteries,
Shared by elders, educating with morals
Myths passed on, most often by orals.

Humankind's emerging, with that Hellenistic dawn
Exploits galore in that past bygone,
Using scant elements, numbering no more than four
Exploiting them all, needing no more.

Air and fire and water and earth
Solved their problems, sometimes with mirth,
Creating civilization, one of the first
And as you'll learn so very well-versed.

On the island of Crete, Minos donned the crown
The problem was, he wore it with frown,
Daedalus and Icarus, both sharing his isle
Rarely could king be found with a smile.

The dad, Daedalus, had a remarkable skill
All he required was a saw and a drill,
Once modeled a gift for the princess of Crete
Which ended up, her most favorable treat.

Minos was greedy, work only for him
Making devices, whatever his whim,
King kept them both stuck in a cave
The pair of them living, just like a slave.

Icarus reaching teens, finding life is a bore
Feeling his oats and wanting much more,
Requesting King Minos to release the youth
Minos says never, and that's the dang truth.

The cave's high up, overlooking the sea
Son consults dad, he's needing to flee,
Hanging from ropes, boy dangles off edge
Collecting some feathers for wings to fledge.

Son's plan, of course, is flying away
If living in France, could wing to Marseille,
Dad suggests, "Don't soar near the ocean,
And if nearing the sun, that's a very bad notion".

The birds seem happy, and the wind is free
Icarus flies carelessly, giddy with glee,
Daring the gulls, let's fly even higher
Freedom forever, from all-possessing sire.

The wings are waxed to keep them secure
If son's not careful, gonna be a short tour,
Mesmerized with joy, subconscious in trance
Too big of a risk, he's forfeited chance.

Reflexes are tardy, teasing his fate
Too close to that orb, responding too late,
The wax is melting, no chance for retreat
If not for his pride, his life could be sweet.

*Daedalus finds Icarus crashed on the sand
Not happy ending the two of them planned,
The lesson this myth has hopefully taught
With too much arrogance, ambition is naught.*

AN UNEXPECTED JOURNEY
....

At the end of Bag End in a nice, cozy hole
Mr. Baggins, a Hobbit, is content with his role
Seven or more traditional meals
And plenty to drink if that's how he feels.

Comfort is dazed, at the door there's a knock
A respected wizard, a bit of a shock,
Then off on adventure with Gandolf the Grey
And thirteen dwarves to enter the fray.

Appointed the 'burglar', confusing at best
Bilbo and mates are off on their quest,
The wizard assures he's got what it takes
They have no idea how big are the stakes.

Soon they are captured by three hungry trolls
Who are looking for meat to fill up their bowls,
Wizard tricks ogres, forgetting the hour
Then turning to stone and losing their power.

Searching troll cave, find weapons galore
Magical blades to outfit the corps,
A dagger for Bilbo, he'll use as a sword
Naming it 'Sting', the burglar has scored.

At elf lord's Rivendell, they've all earned a rest
Elrond advises to help pass their test,
Away to Misty Mountains, find shelter from storm

A cave to dry and a refuge to warm.

The cavern selected is a strong goblin fort
And deep inside is the king and his court,
Gandalf guides dwarves out of harm's way
Leaving poor Bilbo, where he's soon to be prey.

Wandering tunnel, finds strange golden ring
Puts band in his pocket, a magic to bring,
Hissing and whining down by a pool
A creature so eerie, for certain no fool.

He wants to eat stranger, then a contest of wits
Burglar wins match, sending Gollum in fits,
"I'll eat you anyway", Bilbo finding the loop
Hobbit's unseen, can now flee the coop.

Escapes goblins and Gollum, then finding his mates
Soon to discover there's more to their fates,
Out of the frying pan smack into the fire
Escapades becoming more dangerously dire.

Wolf warg howlings sure worry the crew
Evil opponents, right into the stew,
Eagles arrive to rescue the band
Then help from Beorn, a bear and a man.

Company enters Mirkwood, a forest of dread
Bilbo keeps wishing he'd stayed in his bed,
Huge, hairy spiders seeking blood for their life
Arthropods hiding to add to their strife.

The wizard had left to venture alone
Scary spiders to eat them, right to the bone,
The dwarves all tangled in webs that are tight
What they need is a brave, shining knight.

As if their wish was their command
Bilbo to rescue, just like it was planned,
Hobbit's invisible, calls on his 'Sting'
Frees hapless dwarves, unseen with his ring.

Naughty wood elves, never meaning no good
Living real close to that forest, Mirkwood,
Elves seize gang, Bilbo's vanished to eye
He's finally caught on, how to be on the sly.

Prison for the Fellowship seems elves only aim
To dally just now an egregious shame,
Puts mates in barrels, empty of beer
Escape with the river, something to cheer.

Drifting along stream to human Lake Town
Beneath Lonely Mountain hosting snow on its crown,
Now is the time for the burglar to shine
And that my allies, is all by design.

Inside the mountain with the aid of a thrush
All 'round Bilbo, lurks danger's dark brush,
It's the realm of that horrifically, horrific bad dragon
And from the Dwarves treasure, Bilbo filches a flagon.

The Hobbit's unseen and he hasn't been felt

Smaug can't see him, but he can be smelt,
The 'Worm' reveals secret, one scaly is gone
While still retaining the rest of his brawn.

Winged serpent flies away and burns down the town
Nothing is left, it's all turning brown,
But Bard, the archer, has spotted the flaw
And launches his arrow deep into his craw.

Humans and elves want most of the hoard
And all go to war with arrows and sword,
But here come the goblins, wanting it all
Beastly brutes, with plenty of gall.

Elves, dwarves, and humans band together to fight
It's terrible and close, a horrible plight,
At the end of the battle the goblins are dust
Aspiration of enemy has been a big bust.

Returning to Hobbiton, he's back to his hole
Bilbo, the burglar, has finished his goal,
Again, seven meals but never the same
The small, timid Hobbit never again will be tame.

JIM SMILEY AND HIS JUMPING FROG*
. . . .

Simon Wheeler was the garrulous ol'
barman at the Angels Hotel
And the storyteller had the regulars under his spell,
Reputed the best yarn spinner in Angels Camp
Ask the miners, and doves, and even the tramp.

It was the winter of Forty-Nine or the spring of Fifty
The narrator's eyes looked straight,
not the least bit shifty,
The fellers name, let's see, he called hisself Smiley
Carrying on with his tale without emotion, rather dryly.

He was the most curiost man, who just loved to bet
Win or lose, rarely showing no fret,
If there was a dog fight or a chicken
fight, he'd take a chance
He'd take any side, any wager, without even a glance.

If he seen a straddle bug moving, he offered a dare
That ol' boy would foller it to Mexico or anywhere,
Smiley had a mare the boys called fifteen-minute nag
With a three-hunerd yard start, he was ready to brag.

Smiley ketched a frog one day and learned him to jump
Dan'l Webster was a good one, never seemed in a slump,
Keeping him in a lattice box, he'd fetch him to town
Looking for a competition and a wager to lay down.

A stranger arrived in Angels Camp
and had strolled a few blocks
The newcomer looked a grad, from
that school of hard knocks,
He's the best jumper in Calaveras County, Smiley dared
I'd bet ya forty bucks if I had me one
of them, the man declared.

So, Smiley went away to catch a frog in the pond
You could count on the man, his word was his bond,
While Smiley's away, the visitor filled Dan'l with shot
On his return to town, the two frogs ready to squat.

One two three jump! The stranger's frog gave a try
Poor ol' Dan'l Webster just sat there, like he was shy,
The feller took the money and quickly left town
Smiley had a mystery that brought a deep frown.

Why, blame my cats, this boy weighs five pound
Turning Dan'l over, the lead belched on the ground,
He never done ketched that feller,
though he surely done tried
And all Jim Smiley had left was his wounded ol' pride.

Simon Wheeler continued, there oncet
was this yeller, one-eyed cow
Had a tail like a bannaner, but that
was all that time would allow,
It was late and the patrons had heard that one before
And one of the boys at the bar had started to snore.

* Sam L. Clemens, technical advisor

ANIMAL FARM

Another allegory

Manor Farm's most famously, decorated boar
Calls a big meeting for all of the corps.

Old Major had dreamed that all would live free
End human bondage is the heart of his plea.

Beasts of England is launched, as integral hymn
Times will be changing, away from the grim.

Three days later Old Major has died
Manor Farm has lost its top-prized pride.

Napoleon and Snowball and Squealer, young pigs
The three together becoming new bigs.

Animalism's new doctrine to lead the way
Farmer Jones must go, the first in the fray.

Manor Farm's independent, after the brawl
The farm's finally theirs, for each and for all.

With dedicated work, farm prospers at first
Success quickly quenching their liberty thirst.

Snowball is teaching the fauna to read
This can happen when everyone's freed.

Napoleon's tutoring the canine youth
All the principals of Animal Truth.

Farmer Jones reappears to regain his farm
He's well prepared to dish out some harm.

The Battle of Cowshed grows animal pride
Celebrate victory, the pigs have not lied.

Swine are squabbling over future of land
Looking every day like one's to be banned.

Snowball's attacked by Napoleon's gang
Retreating from vicious, clawing and fang.

Last of the meetings, Napoleon's decree
None given choice to dissent or agree.

When plans of Napoleon start going awry
Harsher the measures the chief must apply.

Great Leader rewrites history, sleeping in bed
Drinking good whiskey and becoming a dread.

Animals overworked, returning to same
Pigs spurn acceptance, any blame to their shame.

Most loyal, Boxer, collapses, fully worn,
Animal Farm has failed, a utopian shorn.

Squealer, propagandist, justifying to all,
"Great Leader retains the wisdom of Saul."

Porkers walk upright, now dressing in clothes,
All carry whips adding to throes.

Amended to humans and live as before,
Reverting to folks they had taught to deplore.

BONNIE & CLYDE

Bonnie Parker and Clyde C. Barrow
Destined to bypass the straight and the narrow,
Depression desperados, on the Bureau's roll
Ravage and pillage added to scroll.

Texas bred and in poverty's clutch
But millions survived, without such a crutch,
Criminals petty, they grew from there
Waiting for them, Old Sparky, the chair.

It was Middle America they robbed with their mob
Stores and gas stations working their job,
Looting from banks enhanced their lore
Thirteen murders would define evermore.

It was Bienville Parish, where they met their fate
May of Thirty-four recorded that date,
Motoring a Ford near Gibsland's Woods
Assassination's the end for these two bloodied hoods.

CARNIVORIOUS VULGARIS AND ACCELLERATII INCREDIBUS

This tale has been rated PG 13,
because of violence and nudity.

'Fast and Furry-ous' introduced the pair
Wile E is the rascal, the one with the hair,
And who could forget the bird with fast feet?
And always a beep-beep instead of a tweet.

Coyote's on a hill overlooking the scene
Looking for meat is his fulltime routine,
He spies the bird with his German field glasses
The problem is he's as slow as molasses.

With a napkin in place and with a fork and a knife
The plan is to dine without any strife,
Ambushing prey is on his mind
It's this nice, juicy fowl to which he's inclined.

Wile's stratagem, while watching roadrunner's speed
Cleverly tricking the victim and then feeding his need,
No matter what ruse the coyote employs
Cuckoo reverses the scheme and beep-beeps his noise.

A boomerang and a rocket are useful devices
Carnivore's unconcerned with any of the prices,
Must be an entrepreneur to pay apparatus

Because ACME never offers its products for gratis.

Assembles contraptions to ski clouds and fly
Something always awful happens, and tactics go awry,
Often falling off cliffs, with a puff down below
Or flattened by a bus, the next scene, status quo.

Dramatic displays of creation and focus
Keeps after his nemesis, an insatiable locust,
The big question remaining is for whom do you root?
For me, both adversaries deserve a salute!

If Wily became vegan his life would be easy
Rarely falling off precipices, he would seldom feel queasy,
But he might lose that independence
that helps him create
And aren't we vulgaris all needing that trait?

THE LITTLE RED HEN

another allegory

Red was a Republican, by a chance of fate
Who lived on a farm with friends,
who did little to participate,
Her chums were a yellow duck, a lazy
dog, and a slow, sleepy cat
A dark rumor surfaced that each of
these was a darn Democrat.

One spring day, Red wanted to plant some seeds
Her plan from the beginning was to share the proceeds,
She asked the yellow duck if she would be of assistance
The foul fowl quacked away, adding some distance.

Loafing close by, lazy dog opened an eye
When she asked him for help, never blinked a reply,
One more friend who might help in a pinch
The drowsy cat didn't wake, not moving an inch.

So, the Little Red Hen planted seeds on her own
Her friends, from watching, are tired to the bone,
In a couple months, grain's ready for harvest
The duck was hiding, the dog was absent,
and the cat was the farthest.

When the wheat was cut, all help was refused
Red was depressed and a little bemused,

She walked to the mill, and after grinding the kernels
Back in the barn, she sifted, then wrote in her journals.

The next day, Red was weary and asked for some aid
With rare energy, the trio was playing in glade,
After perusing her cookbooks, Red baked a cake
Smells reached her friends, racing back a mistake.

When all were assembled, Red asked,
'who will help me eat?'
'I will,' quacked, barked, and purred
the duck, dog, and cat in deceit,
'No', said Red. 'I'll eat this solo because I did the work.'
And she pecked the desert, barely hiding a smirk.

THE TAXMAN
....

The Countess of Mercia pled for mercy from taxes
Her husband, the earl, taxes the maxis,
Weary of her entreaties, they strike a harsh bargain
It's all agreed in their olde English jargon.

To ride a horse nude through the Coventry streets
A challenge for Godiva, the elite of elites,
Proclamation is issued: 'Folks remain indoors
Put off for a while all errands and chores'.

With only long hair to protect her from cold
Or sneaky, peeping eyes from those who are bold,
Only one miscreant, a tailor named Tom
He should have studied the Fifty-Ninth Psalm.

Boston held a party in colonial Mass
Their biggest concern was a tea tax impasse,
The Sons of Liberty, the Indian pretenders
King George expected and needed big spenders.

More tariffs to pay, without much of a say
Parliament commanded: Colonials obey,
Into the harbor the tea was tossed
And thanks to that a province was lost.

America's first levy was an excise on whiskey
New government would find taxation is risky,

A resistance is brewed exactly like tea
The folks soon learn that nothing is free.

Henry Thoreau was sent to the slammer
Failure to pay taxes caused most of the clamor,
Like Paine and Jefferson, he espoused the theme
Governments that govern least, the ultimate dream.

Jim Crow, for too long, haunts Dixieland
Failure to pay polls, the Negroes were banned,
Taxes are primeval and as certain as death
And surely, we'll pay, until our last breath.

If you drive a car, I'll tax the street
If you try to sit, I'll tax your seat
If you get too cold, I'll tax the heat
If you take a walk, I'll tax your feet.

George Harrison

A PALATTE

Manfred Albrecht Freiherr von Richthofen,
more simply Red Baron,
Would be easy to rhyme, with a sister named Sharon.

A large, valuable diamond with honorific, Pink Panther,
With Clouseau in charge, we'll soon know the answer.

Black Beauty's a novel, emotes kind and cruel,
Eighteen hundred narrative by Miss Anna Sewell.

Green Hornet fought crime, with his pal by his side,
Britt Reid and Kato most often allied.

Joe Louis is revered as heavyweight champ,
Brown Bomber is found on commemorative stamp.

Purple People Eater's performed, by rocker, Sheb Wooley,
One-eyed and one-horned, it seemed such a bully.

Clockwork Orange, the novel, reflects a dark, scary time,
Just the opposite of noble sublime.

Yellow jackets are wasps, with a sting not a bite,
Disturb a bunch be ready for flight.

Blue Angels streaking the wide blue yonder,
After they pass, they might make you ponder.

During the French Revolution and Reign of Terror,

The Scarlet Pimpernel had no margin for error.

Once upon a time, four lads lived under the seas,
In their yellow submarine, lived lives of ease.

Greg Norman is the tag for golf's white shark,
Very few times was he wide of the mark.

A very nice vodka is produced by the French,
Grey Goose is the brand, a thirst it can quench.

For chartreuse and mauve, it's your turn to try,
You have a go, my brain has run dry.

CITY DITTIES

A is for Adelaide
A city down under,
Plenty of sheilas
Smooth dogs don't blunder.

B is for Berlin
One time divided,
Communism failed
Not all was provided.

C is Cartagena
Plundered by Drake,
Proved the old seadog
Wasn't a fake.

D is for Delhi
Whose folks worship Kali,
She can also be found
On the island of Bali.

E is for Edinburgh
Kilts are the fashion,
Many a lassie
Has expressed her true passion.

F is for Frankfort
Wurst and bier,
Medieval castles

Has no peer.

*G is for Geneva
United Nations and banks,
Neutral forever
No reason for tanks.*

*H is for Helsinki
Land of the saunas,
And the midnight sun
Too cold for piranhas.*

*I is for Iquitos
An Amazon port,
A rainforest town
Rubber barons held court.*

*J is for Jerusalem
One confused city,
Jews, Christians, Muslims
Rule by committee.*

*K is for Kyiv
City not chicken,
Chernobyl,
Sure took a lickin'.*

*L is for London
It's Big Ben, you're hearing,
Watch for Parliament
That's the Thames you're nearing.*

M is for Moscow
Red square's a must,
Quickly see Lenin
There's much to distrust.

N is for Nadi
Found in the Pacific,
Capital of Fiji
To be specific.

O is for Oslo
The Kon Tiki's home,
Thor Heyerdahl for sure
Would still like to roam.

P is for Paris
Tower by Eiffel,
Arc de Triomphe
Surely an eyeful.

Q is for Quito
Found right around zero,
Ask all the gente
Simon's the hero.

R is for Reykjavik
Most northern capital,
Its citizens are cool
And rather unflappable.

S is for Sidney

Opera with sails,
Traces its people,
Back to the jails.

T is for Toledo
A city of Moors,
Might have been mightier
Without Battle of Tours.

U is for Ulan Bator
Genghis was lord,
Mongols, khans, yurts
Were all Yellow Horde.

V is for Vientiane
Just north of Nam,
Now the war's finished
All seems to be calm.

W is for Wellington
Most capital south,
Look for the Maori
With tongue out their mouth.

X is for Xi'an
Where soldiers sleep,
Rise Shi Huang
More mothers to weep.

Y is for Yangon
It's changed its name,
Call it Rangoon
Still is the same.

Z is for Zihuatanejo
Warm Pacific shore,
Pescar y senoritas
Who would want more?

OBTUSE 'HISTERICAL' VERSE

A is for Attila
The Roman scourge,
Legions of Romulus
Could not purge.

B is for Barbary
The pirates of old,
Sailed the Med
For European gold.

C is for Canterbury
Tales of olde,
Penned by Chaucer
Oh! So bolde.

D is for Dali
He painted time,
If he was a poet
He still wouldn't rhyme.

E is for Engels
A partner of Marx,
His statue is seen in
Communist parks.

F is for fascism
The government of Caesar,
Roman and countrymen

Had little leisure.

G is for Gandhi
The resister so passive,
Took from England
A country so massive.

H is for Hindu
A religion with Karma,
Mind the rule
For that would be dharma.

I is for Ivan
That terrible Rus,
So often on Sundays
He made a big fuss.

J is for Jacobins
The purveyors of terror,
Guillotined poor Robespierre
Opps! That was an error.

K is for Kipling
Wrote a poem in a jiff,
Scholars remember
A ditty named 'If'.

L is for Leo
He feuded with Luther,
Gave the Protestants
Hope for the future.

M is for Moors
The Muslims of Spain,
Ruled the vast
Iberian plain.

N is for Napoleon
On Elba he rested,
On return to France
He surely was tested.

O is for Odysseus
An Aegean sailor,
After ten years
He needed a tailor.

P is for patricians
The Roman snobs,
Left the plebes
With lesser jobs.

Q is for Quetzalcoatl
The feathered snake,
Along came Cortes
Proved him a fake.

R is for Red Shirts
Garibaldi's best,
Helped unify Italy
The south and the west.

S if for Socrates
The Athenian teacher,
Swallowed some hemlock,
No potential as preacher.

T is for Turks
Unusually rowdy,
Would chop your head
With never a howdy.

U is for Upanishads
The Hindu bible,
Written in Sanskrit
Originally tribal.

V is for Versailles
The Sun King's home,
A palace so large
All Bourbons could roam.

W is for Waterloo
Napoleon's defeat,
Whipped by the British
With forces elite.

X is for Xerxes
The grandson of Cyrus,
His deeds were told
On paper Papyrus.

Y is for Yin
And also for Yang,
A balance of nature
The religion of Tang.

Z is for Zeus
Olympus was home
His exploits could easily
Fill up a tome.

Another year's over
School is done,
Let's go to the beach
And have some fun!

MUNCHIES

Ogden Nash
Chomped bangers and mash.

Wadsworth Longfellow
Chose cream over jello.

Jonathon Keats
Gobbled carrots and beets.

E.A. Poe
Favored cold sturgeon's roe.

William Blake
Loved the fruit and the flake.

Percy Shelly
Chewed toast with jelly.

Edwin R. Gorsche
Slurped Ukrainian borscht.

If you can pick other poets and food to rhyme
I'll look in my pocket and give you a dime.

HOMO NEANDERTHALIS

Neanderthal is the valley where they first found a hint
Humanlike fossils and bits of a flint,
For decades they were thought to be less than a human
Investigators at first did not use acumen.

Perceived to be cave men, hairy and brutish
Now in hindsight, it all seems so prudish,
Used tools and weapons, all fashioned from stone
Specialists among them found chert to hone.

Their dead were buried with weapon and tool
To deny this fact should bring ridicule,
After all, one must hunt in the life that is next
Without protection, existence perplexed.

Classification finds Neanderthal a genus of Homo
The very same family as Dylon and Como,
The clothes they wore were of animal skins
Wonder if they sported any underpins?

GOLDILOCKS

Once upon a time, way back in the past,
There lived this maid of the lower caste.

Yellow curls galore, serpentining her back,
Pretty as a picture, but an unpleasant quack.

On her inside, and that's our concern,
Never gave a hoot, or three figgys to learn.

A slugabed slacker and one lazy lout,
Lacking all character, there's so little doubt.

She decided one day to walk her lane,
Causing her brain only a bit of a strain.

After two blocks, she elects to snooze,
And there's an empty home, she quickly would choose.

A long nap in the bunks, just for a lark,
Messing all three, leaving her mark.

Porridge in the kitchen, she's enjoyed the spread,
Left dirty dishes, just like her bed!

Mr. and Mrs. Bear with their heir, Baby Bear,
Had saved their money and paid for their fare.

Off to Orlando to enjoy Disney World,
Baby's a cutie, his hair is all curled.

*Returning home, after quite a long drive,
Surely could use forty winks to revive.*

*And then in the morning, a nice bowl of mush,
Then there's Baby, his curls need a brush.*

*Astonished to find, so much had been used,
Security and trust most certainly bruised.*

*"It's gotta be Goldi", said Papa, with frown,
"Reputation is known, all through the town."*

*Next trip's out west to see Disneyland,
And swim in the sea and play on the sand.*

*Next time they'll buy, strong locks for the door
And just to play safe, they'll put tacks on the floor.*

NUDE DUDE

There once lived an emperor, went nutso for clothes,
He had to have duds, so he bought them in droves.

Caring little for his soldiers and not a whit for the folk,
His subjects all thought him, little more than a joke.

Two swindlers arrived and claimed to be weavers,
With invisible threads, they were surely deceivers.

These fraudsters then asked all funds in advance,
Emperor collected taxes, with which to finance.

Charlatans claimed transparency to be of special merit,
And after king paid, his children would inherit.

Wearing new suit, all his ministers agreed,
He's surely a great man and highly pedigreed.

The emperor marched in procession, for all to see,
'How beautiful the suit', folk shouted with glee.

No one would admit they saw nothing at all,
How dignified his attire at this evening's ball.

"He's naked", yelled a child, and they all agreed,
And the emperor carried on, with candor and speed.

RANSOM OF RED CHIEF

Bill and Sam, couple a two-bit-thugs
Better described as wandering slugs,
Entertaining a notion to raise some cash
Adding some bucks to their dwindling stash.

Kicking along to Summit, that Midwestern town
Successful caper should blot out their frown,
Their plan is to kidnap the alcalde's son
Should be a cinch to get this scam done.

The mayor's quite wealthy, but tight as a drum
He's mostly quite ornery and nobody's chum,
When scene is clear they grab the boy
Soon to find, he's surely no toy.

Johnny's pugnacious and makes it a scrap
And all the time, they expected a snap,
Dragged along to their hideout, a cave
Didn't expect their prey to be brave.

Sam to town, Bill and Johnny alone
Returning to sanctum, a painful groan,
Bill is battered and Red Chief's in charge
Never expected an ego so large.

"Bill's to be scalped", the chief demands
"And Sam's to burn", after tying his hands,
Captive and captor have amended position

Reversal of roles, a terrible fission.

*A note to the father, "Two thousand to switch
No problem for you, a man who's so rich",
Drama in cave, increasingly manic
Soon to the point of creating a panic.*

*Back and forth, negotiations fly
The bandits in cave are ready to cry,
The mayor demands two hundred to trade
Not a bad idea, when conditions are weighed.*

*Reprobates pay, escape from their terror
Pause in their flight, relieved of their error,
Never again will they be trying this prank
Might be easier robbing a bank.*

LITTLE RED RIDING HOOD

. . . .

Three years back, Lithuanian scientists
accidentally discovered a time-damaged scroll, with
information pertaining to a missing woman.
They presented the find to the Hans Christian
Andersen Symposium, which meets bi-annually.
The scientists have mysteriously disappeared.

Red lived with Granny, beside a swift stream
Helping the woman churn milk into cream,
Her favorite pet was a cute, furry pup
Feeding him scraps and watching him sup.

The crony's aged badly, all grumpy and mean
Skinny and green like an ol' string bean,
At the same pace, Red's gained beauty of face
But without even one, redeemable grace.

The pup has grown into one, vicious brute
Remember that fleecy, adorable coot?
Creatures spoke same, in those old, olden days
The two scheme a plan, Gran's out in a blaze.

Wolf eats Gran, leaves only few bones
Easy to hide, just under some stones,
Free and clear to share her home
Still feeling cramped, needing more room to roam.

Down the road and over two knolls
Nice, grassy meadow, would meet their goals,
And by the way, there are three small digs
Guess what? Yup, they're the Three Little Pigs!

ELEMENTARY, MY DEAR WATSON
....

(Never appeared in any of A. C. Doyle's
sixty Sherlock Holmes stories)

The Thin Man, Nick Charles, is married to Nora
An aristocrat heiress with plenty of aura,
Dashiell Hammett, with his flip repartee
Created these trappings of rich bourgeois.

Sam Spade's another persona private eye
Detective deduces all on the sly,
Fat man Greenstreet and the lovely Miss Astor
Seduced the gumshoe, but never his master.

Elderly spinster, created by Christie
Plots all evolving most misty and twisty,
Clever Miss Marple lives in vill, Mary Mead
Suspects should have quit and run from their greed.

Fu Manchu was a very bad man
Always having most dastardly plan,
Charlie Chan to the rescue, he'd foil that scheme
With Number One Son, spoiling Fu's theme.

Reformed safecracker and most clever thief
Malefactor's turned over, an honest new leaf
Friend to those who have no friends
Boston Blackie's turned straight and making amends.

Author Conan Doyle, at the turn of the century
Created Sherlock Holmes to fill penitentiary,
He stuffed his pipe and played violin
Never inconvenienced with any chagrin.

Nancy Drew and those clever boys, Hardy
Deciphered crooks like a Master Leonardi,
Still in school and players of sport
Sent many a bad guy to police and then court.

User of technology with clever aplomb
Never took a bribe, never greasing his palm,
Clever Tess Truehart's this cop's true love
Dick Tracy and she, going hand with a glove.

Clumsy inspector slogs Surete de French
Thinks like a hammer and deems like a wrench,
Klutzy but persistent, Clouseau will prevail
Our hero ends up, putting bad guys in jail.

Frank Drebin's a sleuth, always seeming to bungle
Misdeeds in either the city or jungle,
"Like a midget at a urinal, had to stand on my toes"
And with that bit of info, I'll come to a close.

MONSTER MASH
. . . .

Lights flashed nightly from the old castle's tower
Burghers remember, and the oldest would cower.

Back to ancestral home, after living abroad
Victor's son still wonders, why the research is flawed?

With Igor's assistance and insight to contrive
Culminates in laboratory with shouted, "It's alive".

Lawrence Talbot must travel to visit his clan
Called on Sir John, which was part of his plan.

An evening's outing found Gypsy's in camp
A Welsh full moon, foggy and damp.

On the way home, Larry's bitten by beast
Fortuneteller explained his real life has ceased.

"When the moon is full and the Wolfbane bloom
You will change to wolf and find souls to doom".

Deep in Transylvania a citadel looms
Cold, dreary misty it appears in the glooms.

If you look to the rampart, a bat will fly
Before dawn's light, a mortal must die.

When hunting this fiend, take a strong wooden stake
By day he must slumber and will not be awake,

Open his casket...be ready...hammer deep
He's changed his grave, and tonight he will creep.

The Invisible Man dresses in bandage with shade
Traveling around, he has police to evade.

Chemist Jack Griffin had a scientist passion
Ingesting monocane, he no longer needs fashion.

Driven mad by the drug, he must dominate world
Naarcotic brain cogitated, and this idea had all swirled.

Hiding in a barn on a cold winter's night
Footprints in the snow and the cops followed flight.

SWEET CAROLYN
....

She was a knockout babe, and not a little bit shy
On her first day on campus, she's the apple of our eye,
And not just the faculty, her students would agree
And there she was, all footloose and free.

She shared 105, she was firm, she was fair
If anyone was naughty, all it took was a glare,
Psychology was her subject, but she taught much more
With respect for her kids, she earned that rapport.

That day we cried, we lost our favorite gal
She was so much more than a friend and a pal,
Funny and bold and saucy and sweet
All the above, not a hint of conceit.

Carolyn retired after a whole bunch of years
She will always bring smiles, she will always bring tears,
But she really hasn't left us, just look in your soul
With loyalty to friends, she's filled her final scroll.

You can take the girl from Kentucky,
but not Kentucky from the girl
If you didn't look closely, you would
swear she's Minnie Pearl,
Carolyn was a Ranch Hand, the best of them all
She cain't hep it, the fault's in her drawl.

Sweet Caroline

Good times never seemed so good
Sweet Caroline
I believed they never could
Sweet Caroline
Good times never seemed so good

Neil Diamond

GREATEST GENERATION

∙ ∙ ∙ ∙ ∙ ∙ ∙ ∙ ∙ ∙

The Roaring Twenties, after four years of war
Folks living lives with abundance galore,
The crash was felt, October Twenty-Nine
Ended the good times with a bold underline.

Bubble burst Black Thursday, with economic fears
Fat cat investors all shedding their tears,
Rumors ran rampant all through this land
For most of the folk, not a hint of a plan.

End of affluence, fifteen million unemployed
Half the banks failed, business destroyed,
Then a president's elected, with a hope and a goal
Alphabet agencies helped us out of the hole.

Bread lines and soup kitchens, apples for a cent
Stand in line for a handout, no way to pay rent,
Then a six-year dust bowl caused by a drought
Ecological catastrophe brought more of a doubt.

Movies served as shrinks and for only a dime
Lose self in a film, few hours at a time,
Escape folks asking, "Brother, got an extra nickel?"
For many in the crowd, their lives seemed so fickle.

FDR's New Deal brought short term relief
Some help for the workingman, pausing from grief,
Most folks were wearied, Prohibition's repealed

That social experiment never really appealed.

Nineteen Thirty-Nine, finest year for the screen
Seemed the perfect tonic, when the times were so lean,
Stagecoach and Din, produced with real feeling
Dorothy and Toto were also appealing.

That Day of Infamy brought war to The States
One of America's most epochal dates,
The Empire of Japan in that dastard attack
At the harbor of Pearl, a stab in the back.

Arising to fight from deep Depression den
Eighteen-year-old boys soon to be men,
Normandy, Bastogne, the Fighting 442
Guadalcanal and Peleliu, to name just a few.

Return from the war to build a new life
Never to complain, no matter the strife,
"It was my job, heroes never came back",
They've earned a toast, with a tumbler cognac.

I was a small boy and witnessed some of this
My brother-in-law served, then married to my sis,
Continue to thank and honor this clan
They deserve our respect, every woman, every man.

SAY IT AIN'T SO, JOE

He never learned to write because
he never learned to read
Those skills weren't required, for him to succeed,
At six, he toiled a twelve-hour shift
Small wages he earned gave his family a lift.

The mill where he worked sported a semi-pro team
At thirteen years, a ballplayer's dream,
Couldn't read from the menus, ordered what others chose
"That's a good idea, I'll have one of those."

Contests on weekends paid two bucks a game
At the turn of the century, he was gaining acclaim,
Played without shoes one day, on hot blistered feet
Acquired a moniker, never missing a beat.

'Shoeless' Joe Jackson began his career
And soon to become a player premier,
.408 batting in his rookie season
Flawless in the field was another good reason.

Then World Series champs in Seventeen
The White Sox won, Jackson's part of the scene,
Black Betsy's his bat, while he guarded left field
Few hits to his area, never much of a yield.

Joe worked in a shipyard the following season
World War One was a pretty good reason,

Real drama began with the '19 World Series
Cincy triumphed, which started the queries.

The Reds were underdogs, which didn't surprise
Suspicious folks thought, games must be a guise,
A grand jury convened to test allegation
Sporting world's saddened by sinful sensation.

Joe hit .375, played field without error
Twelve hits established a World Series terror,
Jury then acquitted the 'Black Sox' Eight
A hundred years later, it still stirs debate.

Landis imposed a lifetime ban
Innuendo and rumor, not proof for the fan,
In the Field of Dreams, Joe played once more,
Do you think that's enough, to even the score?

BULLY

On the first of July, eighteen hundred ninety-eight
'Pecos Bill' Shafter, the general, is earning his fate.

Under tropical sun, commanding that ragtag brigade
All were brave, most were afraid.

On the top of the hill, Spanish guns barred their climb
Young soldiers on both sides, still in their prime.

Under brutal barrage, many hundreds fell
No time to mourn and say farewell.

Buffalo Soldiers and cowboys and some college men
The Spaniards repelled them time and again.

But the order of the day: "Take San Juan Hill"
All that carnage, such a bitter pill.

Gunfire rained down on the troops below
Then the order came, "Climb and reach that plateau".

TR led his Rough Riders up that slope
Most horses left behind no way they could cope.

By the end of the day, both sides in a haze
Along with the fatigue, mostly malaise.

The newspapers reported a stunning success
With all those casualties it seemed in excess.

*Returning home heroes, with a charismatic colonel
Press praising Rough Riders in everyone's journal.*

*Teddy took his place, as president twenty-six
He mostly spoke softly, while carrying big sticks.*

FUED FOOLS

The Tug Fork of the Sandy is where all of this starts
The Hatfield's and McCoy's are the two counterparts.

West Virginia and Kentucky were the venues concerned
Every slight and every insult heatedly returned.

'Devil Anse' Hatfield and 'Ole Ran' McCoy
They loathed each other like Greece hated Troy.

One fought for Blue and the other for Gray
That was the start of kinship's decay.

Honor and justice and revenge, of course
Throughout the decades there's been no remorse.

The families united for Family Feud
Wouldn't be surprised if more trouble was brewed!

BAY STATE

From Plymouth to Plymouth, the Mayflower sailed
With courage and faith, these pilgrims prevailed,
The Wampanoag Algonquians were there to aid
Helped these newcomers, apprehensions allayed.

The Puritans arrived second, to escape persecution
Massachusetts Bay Colony's the perfect solution,
Let's skip some time, to a history that's hearty
I'm sure you remember the Boston Tea Party.

Radical Sam Adams stirred up the crowd
Make-believe Indians at the harbor powwowed,
Into the sea, English tea was tossed
No matter the consequence, no matter the cost.

The small town of Salem is famous for witches
When brought to trial there were plenty of snitches,
Mass hysteria spread and the final result
Sorceress hung high for devil's occult.

Massachusetts set the stage that changed our nation
From subjects to citizens, extraordinary inspiration,
At Thanksgiving time all the puritans prayed
Now, it's the touchdowns the Patriots have made.

LITTLE GREEN MEN

Back in thirty-eight with radio only
A dark, stormy night and the mean streets were lonely,
Mercury Theatre on a Halloween eve
A broadcast for listeners to misconceive.

Some turned on late and were surprised to hear
The Martians had landed and were very, very near,
Orson Welles had altered the tale by Wells
A portrait in horror in which Wells excels.

Allegedly, mass panic had scourged this land
Green Martian hordes, unable to withstand,
Panic in the streets and cities afire
Folks all thinking, it was their time to expire.

Updated news bulletins of the alien invasion
Prompted the citizens to find some evasion,
Others were listening to The Bergen Show
Some felt cheated, missing the Welles' tableaux.

OVER THE RAINBOW

Warblers soar over the White Cliffs of Dover
If a watcher of birds, collect your composure,
Look for the bluebirds of World War Two
I think they go tweet instead of a moo.

Family Diomedeidae claim the mighty albatross
Never be confused, with the American sloth,
One is a mammal, the other a bird
One is feathered, the other is furred.

The stork sports a sword and has long, skinny legs
Its frogs and snakes, and wormys it begs,
They live in the wetlands away from the shire
Will rubbing their legs, start a warm fire?

On the dry, open steppes you might find the bustard
Colored grey and brown, with a slight touch of mustard,
Preferring the land, they're the heaviest bird
Omnivorous in fact but snakes are preferred.

Home, home on the range, where the
deer and the antelope play
The Prairie Chicken, in spring,
puts on a courting display,
Kinda looks like the bop or the herky jerky
But it may be a grouse or maybe a turkey.

The poor Dodo's extinct, makes it hard to find
They looked rather clumsy and poorly designed,
Aepyornithidae has also departed
Makes one wonder, why it even was started?

In St. Louis and Phoenix, a Cardinal plays ball
Athletics carried on in that fast, urban sprawl,
Beautiful redbird, with a cute little comb
Flashing real pretty on top of its dome.

Charlie Parker was the jazz master, without a peer
There was none better, within his sphere,
"Don't play the sax, let it play you"
If you heard 'The Bird', you would count it a coup.

Way down south, where it is really, really cold
There lives a brave bird that is really, really bold,
Can't fly in the air, does super in the sea
Which seems to be an idiosyncrasy.

The bat's not a bird and at night's high strung
Just 'cause she's got fur and nurses her young,
She flies in the evening and can get in your hair
Insects and fruit are mostly her fare.

"Yes, yes, my little chickadee", a line from W.C.
Birds are a treasure, yes siree, yes siree',
Chick-a-dee-chick-a-dee is the song they sing
A lovely little bird when out on the wing.

*Some birds are called chicks, and some are called sheilas,
Might want to court some, with beers or tequilas.
Senorita or fraulein, or twist and twirl,
I'd take a chance and give them a whirl.*

HAVE GUN----WILL TRAVEL
∙ ∙ ∙ ∙ ∙ ∙ ∙ ∙ ∙

Paladin took the name of a Charlemagne knight
Very gentlemanly and mostly upright,
Mercenary gunfighter with a Robin Hood hype
Helped most folks with a legitimate gripe.

Ensconced in Frisco's Carlton Hotel
And on his arm most often a belle,
When on an assignment, he travelled the West
Helping the citizens so often oppressed.

Bat Masterson was a marshal, a gambler, a dandy
With derringer in vest, he was more than just handy,
Always a fancy dude, preferring a cane
A character of the time, seeming urbane.

For women and adventure, he travelled the West
Challenging the bad guys while remaining well-dressed,
With derby hat, black jacket, vest, and a tie
The ladies in towns never short of supply.

The Cartwright's were featured in the series, Bonanza
Their ranch, the Ponderosa, a huge extravaganza,
Three sons were sired, by thrice widowed Ben
Each one quite different, with a lot to commend.

Cisco and Pancho, duet desperados
As tales were told they became aficionados,
The Cisco Kid's one heroic caballero

Looked the part, with his wide-brimmed sombrero.

Diablo and Loco were our heroes' steeds
Like Silver and Scout, they aided good deeds,
'Quicksilver Murder' and especially 'Big Switch'
Exciting episodes portrayed to enrich.

Davey, Davey Crocket, King if the Wild Frontier
Were stories portrayed about a real pioneer,
Davey killed a bear with only his knife
In strife, the animal seemed larger than life.

Off to Washington to represent in the House
Ideas and ideals with which to espouse,
Later at the Alamo, he stood his ground
As Mexican cannon balls exploded around.

F Troop was a satire of the wild, wild West
Slapstick comedy and burlesque at its best,
Chronically clumsy, with a captain most gallant
He tried really hard, but lacked army talent.

Honest Matt Dillon was a Dodge City marshal
The justice he brought was always impartial,
Gunsmoke revolved around Chester and Kitty
He had a limp, and she was quite pretty.

Dime novel dramas of western, epic lore
Cowboy fiction to appreciate evermore,
Ned Buntline, Zane Grey, and L' Amour would agree
Long-lasting series deserves pedigree.

Kung Fu was different, featured action martial arts
Spread hermit wisdom with vanquishing smarts,
Kwai Caine toured the west as a Shaolin monk
Preconceived ideas he would bravely debunk.

Twenty Mule Team Borax sponsored Death Valley Days
Told wonderful stories, when the West was ablaze,
The programs were hosted by that crusty, 'Old Ranger'
We watched him each week, he was never a stranger.

Western drama, Reagan's last work as an actor
A political career, his very next chapter,
The stories were based on an actual event
Then the star of the show's elected president.

'A cloud of dust and a hearty Hi-yo, Silver, away'
Meant a whole lot more than a worn cliché,
The Ranger along with his faithful pal, Tonto
Chased bad guys to justice, faster than pronto.

The Ranger's kemosahbe, played by Jay Silverheels
Was his loyal compadre through all their ordeals,
Stranger used silver bullets and a horse by that name
"Who was that masked man", some would exclaim.

THE GENERAL

Treebeard was astute, the oldest to endure
Venerable for sure and very mature,
Middle-Earth was his home, his home on the range
Being an Ent at that time, not really that strange.

They were huge, they were smart,
they could walk if they wished
There was many an orc that got himself squished,
They are mostly gone, but some still thrive
Over there in Sequoia if you feel like a drive.

He yawned when he saw his original dawn
And there close by was a cute, spotted fawn,
They looked at each other, then the deer sprang away
Kinda interesting for a sapling's first day.

It was crowded below; he knew he needed light
That orb up there, seducing and bright,
He stretched really strong, but so did his mates
Only the heartiest would win, just one of their fates.

Instinct prevailed, he had something grand
All on his own, without helping hand,
A hundred years later, he was tall for his age
And all that had happened could fill up a page.

He was firmly in the ground when Jesus taught
Stretching high in the air, when the religions all fought,
Atheists and Christians, Muslims, and Jews
So much in common, some customs and views.

Of course, he didn't know it, but history's been written
All over the world, not only in Britain,
The Romans had yet to conquer that isle
That would take place, in a bit of a while.

Two thousand years later, he's climbing quite tall
All taking place in that vast, Sierra sprawl,
His bark is red, and his roots are strong,
But with fire and man, something bad could go wrong.

The wheel invented the auto, brings folks from afar
To see this mansion and real superstar,
General Sherman's still growing, still reaching for sky
And if you are silent, you might hear a slight sigh.

SATCHEL THE SAIGE

Leroy was a man of indeterminate age
And never the one to take the backstage,
"How old are you, Satch", would come the question
"Better ask my ma", he relayed a suggestion.

The nickname, Satchel, invented by friend
Carrying bags at the station, gave him money to spend,
Into some trouble, before thirteen
Learned his lesson to keep his nose clean.

The Mobile Tigers, his semi-pro team
Struck out opponents like a vanishing cream,
Chattanooga's the club in the Negro League
Dispensing most batters, without a fatigue.

There's many a legend of Satchel's success
One thing for certain, a batters' distress,
Opposing Dizzy Dean, while in Dean's prime
Satch won that game, on borrowed time.

Dominican Republic, Puerto Rico, and Cuba
Satch threw that spheroid like a power-bazooka,
Pitched Negro World Series, a Kanas City Monarch
The inspired Paige had reached a new hallmark.

At age forty-two, signed a major league deal
Forty thousand dollars, a really big steal,
The Cleveland Indians was the team to finance
After Robinson and Doby had joined the 'Big Dance'.

Infectious and cocky, a pop entertainer
Pitching without rest, a graceful campaigner,
Satchel Paige's been inducted to the Hall of Fame
A fitting tribute, for the ol' ballgame.

Satchel pitched a game at age fifty-nine
Throwing smartly, he laid it out on the line,
"Age is a question of mind over matter,
If you don't mind, it sure doesn't matter".

DA BISCUIT
. . . .

This unlikely champ became a symbol of hope
Giving Depression folk some reason to cope,
Foaled in Lexington in year thirty-three
Began his career as a soft wannabe.

Failing to win first seventeen races
Seemed little potential with only mild chases,
Sold to Tom Howard for eight thousand dollars
Considered rather foolish by astute, racing scholars.

Unorthodox training brought the Biscuit success
New owner, Howard, had problems to redress,
Trainer, Tom Smith, with jockey, Red Pollard
Raced this stallion that was now rarely collared.

Nineteen Thirty-Seven and the
trendy 'Hundred Grander'
Santa Anita was filled for the patrons to gander,
Competitor, Rosemont, won by a nose
Fans at home, followed on their radios.

Seabiscuit's top money winner in thirty-seven
'Horse of the Year' honors would seem closer to heaven,
War Admiral won 'Crown', that very same year
A match race would feature, two horse's premier.

Forty thousand in attendance and
forty million listening
Forty thousand palms were wet, and
their faces were glistening,
For 'Match of the Century', Pimlico's the host
Winner of race could officially boast.

The betting was fierce, with The Admiral the choice
And many in attendance would own a hoarse voice,
Jockey Pollard was out, previously hurt
George Woolf taking over and riding alert.

Seabiscuit broke first, at the sound of the bells
For over a mile, they raced like gazelles,
War Admiral was game, and raced his best time
Howard's stallion by four lengths and a feeling sublime.

In Thirty-eight, Biscuit's earned 'Horse of the Year'
These winning ways building legendary career,
But a ligament injury put the horse on hold
Pollard and the steed together paroled.

The 'Hundred Grander' again, for that coveted prize
Santa Anita once more for the fans to surmise,
Seventy-eight thousand in a wild disarray
Witnessed dramatic finish, Biscuit's won the day.

Competing eighty-nine times with a warrior's heart
He'll remain that special athlete, who is held apart,
Retired to stud, sired hundred eight foals
Only two who met the new owner's goals.

*Shirley Temple and Hillenbrand both told this story
Of this unlikely champ and all of his glory,
Seabiscuit's deeds deliver a fine inspiration
Just a bit a luck and a bucket of perspiration.*

BRIGHT PATH

Wa-Tho-Huk was his Sac and Fox name
Meet Jim Thorpe, name's one and the same.

His story begins in Pottawatomie, Oklahoma
Attended college at Carlisle, to earn a diploma.

Nineteen and seven commenced his career
It was competitive sports to which he'd adhere.

Football, basketball baseball, and track
Even ballroom dancing, always ahead of the pack.

Running back, defense, punter, or kicker
He was a little bit stronger and a heck of a lot slicker.

Legendary coach Warner mentored his star
Won National Championships, exemplar.

Awarded All American in eleven and twelve
Many more trophies for him to shelve.

President Eisenhower remarked, when he was cadet
"Jim Thorpe had a lot of get up and get".

Stockholm hosted those Olympic Games
International respect burst into flames.

Pentathlon, decathlon, Thorpe won the gold
Unbelievable achievement, he'd broken the mold.

Before the Games he played baseball for pay
Reported as little as two dollars a day.

Stripped of his medals and labeled professional
Some American newspapers had made it obsessional.

Thorpe then played baseball for the New York Giants
Also St. Louis, as one of their clients.

He toured the world with Major League players
Shaking hands with emperors, the kings, and the mayors.

The Brewers and Cubs, two more of his squads
Filling the parks and beating the odds.

Also stellar in the Football League
Always played hard, showing little fatigue.

Jim Thorpe's gold medals were finally restored
The original ruling was always abhorred.

A quote from King Gustav was quite replete
'You, Sir, are the world's greatest athlete!'

BUCCANNEERS
. . . .

Captain Kidd wielded both pistols and cutlass
Escaped from the English, would've
brought him to justice,
Buried baubles and gewgaws and much of his treasure
To return at retirement for leisure and pleasure.

Edward Teach 'Blackbeard' braving two sharp swords
Defeated the Scarborough which angered the lords,
Captured near Virginia it was off with his head
Placed on a pike to prove he was dead.

Bartholomew Roberts, sobriquet Back Bart
Considered at the time as astute as Descartes,
Plundered successfully four hundred ships
With a looming boldness, a near apocalypse.

Anne Bonne quaffed rum, and fought most profusely
Comportment and morals, she showed off most loosely,
Captured with her crew, she's sentenced to hang
During her trial she was plagued with harangue.

Sir Henry Morgan, a freebooter, preyed on the Spanish
They tried with their squadrons to harm and to banish,
Knighted by King Charles, he settled Caribbean
Does that make him an Indo-European?

Sir Francis Drake, a most lauded 'Sea Dog'
The Spanish wasting reals to seize him and flog,
First English mariner to circle the globe
Sailed America's west coast to peer and to probe.

Cheung Po Tsai, Asian pirate renown
Captured ships of his realm and many a town,
Harassed and captured, by the sailors of Qing
Then worked for the emperor, more riches to bring.

Ching Shih commanded 80,000 men
She robbed for Yuan and for silver and Yen,
Awarded pirate amnesty for peace on the seas
Then managed a brothel, living with ease.

BONNIE & CLYDE

Bonnie Parker and Clyde C. Barrow
Destined to bypass the straight and the narrow,
Depression desperados, on the Bureau's roll
Ravage and pillage added to scroll.

Texas bred and in poverty's clutch
But millions survived, without such a crutch,
Criminals petty, they grew from there
And waiting for them, Old Sparky, the chair.

It was Middle America they robbed, with their mob
Stores and gas stations, working their job,
Looting from banks, enhancing their lore
Thirteen murders would define evermore.

It was Bienville Parish, where they met their fate
May of '34, recorded that date,
Motoring a Ford, nearing Gibsland Woods
Assassination's the end for these two bloodied hoods.

'ANOTHER FINE MESS'
....

The Long Ranger needed Tonto, and Costello bedeviled Abbott,
Their kookiest tomfoolery became such a habit.

Hope partnered Crosby, while Tom chased Jerry,
Made 'em laugh in the hills, as well as the prairie.

Bonnie robbed banks with her boyfriend, Clyde,
While Jekyll and Hyde were intimately allied.

Historically speaking, Lee opposed Grant,
And sometimes an uncle might have an aunt.

From the Roaring Twenties through World War Two,
This duo familiar, as a favorite old shoe.

Stanley's mostly childlike and rather naïve,
Always 'in a jam' with a trick up his sleeve.

Ollie played the smarter one, that Stan often bested,
In all their slapstick, they're both sorely tested.

Hardy was heavy and the skinny one, Laurel,
With all their foolishness, most often a quarrel.

They're a dopey duo, with an aura that's noble,
A lasting popularity that certainly seems global.

Hundred three steps with piano on back,
Helped America chuckle; they had that knack.

In the dark, depression days when folks needed laughs,
They could watch The Boys, with their innocent gaffes.

"What other type of ice cream don't you have",
Such a clever line, and it works like a salve.

It's time to watch zany, 'Way out West',
It's Laurel and Hardy at their very, very best.

Both of these sidekicks remain so immortal,
Stan and Ollie always earning a chortle.

'GET YOUR KICKS'
....

If you ever make a plan to motorcar west,
Take that ol' road, that the song says is best.

There's a jingle 'bout a journey, it's a song you all know,
The towns of this tune suggest a motor tableau.

On you mark it's Chicago, revered for their Cubs,
The Billy Goat Tavern's just one of the pubs.

Saint Looey is famed for the Arch and their ball,
The Cardinals usually challenge, especially in Fall.

Joplin got a visit, from Bonnie and Clyde,
The duo divested banks, unhappy to provide.

Oklahoma City's kinda' pretty, and
home of The Thunder,
And if you don't stop, you'll most probably wonder.

Amarillo is where it oughta be, smack on the handle,
Renown for just regular folks, not used to much scandal.

Gallup offers steaks, at their Badland Grill,
If you're a pensive vegan, drink two pints and chill.

Flagstaff's rather modern, but echoes rugged past,
At the Phillips 66, get your vehicle gassed.

Winona's out of sequence, if you follow with map,
Careful with your tempo, watch for speeder's trap.

After Kingman there's California, just 'cross that line,
Look for golden poppies on their welcoming sign.

Coming on to Barstow, I suggest you hurry through,
Drive two miles, and salute 'em, adieu.

You're a veteran of the road, when reaching San Berdoo,
It's as good a place as any, if you gotta use the loo.

Your journey will be finished on the Santa Monica pier,
And don't you dare forget, a T-shirt souvenir.

If it's ready, steady, go...get into the mix,
Go get your kicks...on Route Sixty-Six.

IL MILIONE
....

Venice said caio, in twelve fifty-four
His years of travel would bring mighty lore,
Trained by his family, of a merchant class
Many adventures he would amass.

Niccolo and Maffio, his uncles, would mentor
Historical legends very soon he would enter,
Away into Asia through the winding Silk Road
By horse and by camel, Marco's goods often flowed.

It seemed improbable for the vast Holy Empire
That a competing culture could also aspire,
But Cathay was huge with riches galore
Surprised the West and they had to explore.

The great khan's lure seduced from the East
Stories by uncles on return were unleashed,
Marco's career, caravan to court
Precious goods to guard and safely transport.

The Pamirs were fearsome and the Gobi's formidable
Water, food, and weather were often deplorable,
By the end of the path, they had travelled four years
Xanadu's magnificent but elicits some fears.

Seventeen years the three Polo's wandered
Language and music were mores they pondered,
Permission was given and the Polo's departed
A long way back, from where they had started.

Leaving by sea, they chanced a typhoon
Over the decks many bodies were strewn,
Into this melee many wayfarers lost,
Into the storm many pilgrims were tossed.

Arriving in Turkey, they're plundered with pleasure
Almost home, they're robbed of their treasure,
Two decades plus, finally Venice at last
But there's too little time to ponder the past.

In a war versus Genoa, Marco commanded a boat
He is captured and sentenced to prison remote,
Rustichello's an author, who shared his cell
Wrote down the tales that Marco would tell.

A Million Lies was perused by the folk
But Marco's marvels were considered a hoax,
Receiving recognition only after his death
Marco Polo claimed candor, until his last breath.

FAIR DINKUM
. . . .

Indigenous Australians arrived a long time ago
They lived on the plain and on the plateau,
Aborigines thrived without iron or the wheel
The way they flourished seems very ideal.

Dreaming was the sacred era,
brought forth their Creation
Animist mythology, their sacred causation,
The Didgeridoo, in its own way unique
Except to the domestics who understand its mystique.

First European landing was by
the Dutchman, Janszoon
Who beat James Cook, which was so opportune,
On the Briton's recommendation,
Botany Bay was founded
English jails provided folk, who settled unbounded.

But the Catholic Irish were a cause for concern
Political prisoners, they mostly were spurned,
Gold rushes and bushrangers, a colorful past
An interesting history for the enthusiast.

Two world wars, Vietnam, and more
Our friend's underneath, loyal to core,
Anzac Day's a remembrance, of every campaign
First to join in the battle, while remaining humane.

Two ripper Olympiads they've been proud to host
Went so smoothly they've the right to a boast,
The Australian Open is something to brag
And Henley-on-Todd should add to their swag.

Oz is a delight, with beaches supreme
Paradise on the Gold Coast, a surfboarder's dream,
Don't miss Uluru, Aboriginal sacred site
Plan some time there, with an overnight.

In Sydney, catch an opera in the house with the sails
Off the shore, if you're lucky, you might see some whales,
Put Cairns on your list, and explore that coast
Dive that Barrier Reef, find a reason to boast.

Platypus and wombat and the blue tongue lizard
To find these creatures doesn't take such a wizard,
Camels and roos, and that Tasmanian Devil
A first-class experience and that's on the level.

Kangaroo Island and Darwin, in the Territory
Plan a trip to the continent, it's most obligatory,
Coopers Pale Ale is one of their beers
All you have to remember is, "G'day' and 'Cheers".

RUN BEAR, RUN

My doggie-chum, his name was Beau
Wagged his tail to say hello.

Loyally devoted and trusting friend
He gave his all, to help Jo mend.

Beau walked with us at java time
Just like he did when in his prime.

Played on the beach with George, his dad
He was to him, a true comrade.

So many friends, he met with wags
Just like the breeze that blows the flags.

A visit each night to my abode
Swishing his tail, his cheer bestowed.

When the mailman delivered, Beaumont would scowl
Protecting us all with his warning growl.

Endearingly called Bear by Jo, his love
The two so tight, just like a glove.

"Run, Bear, run", Jo's gleeful shout
Just like the wind, so little doubt.

Beaumont's left us, to play and to rest
Over the years, our pal's proved the best.

"Run, Bear, Run"

Grampa Jim

JOHNNY

Ms. Jones asked Johnny to name his favored animal
Teacher considered his answer quite cannibal,
"Fried chicken of course", his honest response
Third grader answered with a real nonchalance.

The next day, another question,
and she seemed rather sad
"What's your favorite animal alive", quizzing the lad,
"Chicken of course", and she asked him why?
"Because you can eat 'em, and that's no lie".

Off to the office for a bit of advice
Expecting from the headmaster some serious chastise,
Mr. McMasters thought, it was all kinda funny
Advised Johnny not to think so much with his tummy.

The third day, Ms. Jones asked a historical question
Johnny's response seemed to cause her aggression,
"Which favorite person do you admire the most"?
"Colonel Sanders", he replied…principal's office new post.

MORE STOOPID STUFF

A man served burgers in ol' Victorville
Sandwiches he sold straight from his till,
I ordered a double
He said, "That's no trouble",
So, I gave him a three-dollar bill.

There once was a gal named Mindia
Whose boyfriend worked in India,
Living 'cross the seas he was hard to please
So, he stayed in Mau counting rupees.

Have you heard about the girl from Maine,
Who loves to drink fine champagne?
After four sips, she discovers rapport,
Then, she's hard to ignore.

My favorite fan dancer, Sally Rand
Arabs love to watch here firsthand,
She once met a sheik, while whirling in Saudi
And was asked to gyrate quite bawdy.

There once was a scholar from Munich
Whose job was to probe mystic Runic,
Baffled by ciphers, she'd drink zwei bier
Which would make those Norse letters clear.

One time a gondolier from Venice
Wished to play some serious tennis,
But he used his oar instead of a racket
Maybe that's why he earned a low bracket.

Once upon a time in Pomona
Dwelled a swervy, curvy persona,
When she went outside, she would forget her clothes
You could hear the "yea buddies" and "ohhs".

Remember gregarious Gertrude?
All over her body was tattooed,
Portrayed some scenes of lusty maneuver
She was painted in downtown Vancouver.

Celesse, she prospered in Brussels
She was famous for very nice muscles,
Working out at the gym, with big heavy weights
She was stronger than most of her dates.

There once was a gypsy from Bristol
Unfortunately, she lost her rare crystal,
She tried tarot and read some palms
She was relegated to begging for alms.

Fatima had a boyfriend from Durban
His curry she wrapped in his turban,
At lunchtime, she most frequently worried
That his hair made samosas quite furried

Yoko lived just a bit south of Tokyo
Her ichiban doll was Pinocchio,
Cuddling closely, she collected some splinters
But sandpaper helped in the winters.

The bearded lady was considered quite shady
When she married that Shamus O'Grady,
After shaving her face, she resembled her mother
So, they pretended that each was the other.

The pirate had one wooden leg
A realio trulio rotten egg,
Left hand a hook and he wore a glass eye
With a cutlass tied to his thigh.

Octopuses live in da wadda
Do they remember deyr mudda and fadda?
Wit all dem arms or are is dey legs
Do you think they tromp on their eggs?

The Little Prince when exploring Sahara
Found that desert a sharp firma terra,
Giving his aviator a gifts of the stars
Helped ease those heartbreaking scars.

One time a man from old town Prague
Dreamed he was kissing his favorite dog,
After awakening from fantasy, just after first light
He was glad his dog didn't bite.

Lovely Meilani tends bar in Tahiti
After work, she offends with graffiti,
After all her patrons have gone off to bed
Mei paints Papeete bright red.

Rosey Rosenkranz gets ants in her pants
When she sits on those sticky green plants,
Always a scratch when she gets the itch
She needs Abercrombie and Fitch.

Syrup is slower in winter
But in summertime, it turns into sprinter,
Why doesn't our insides ever feel sticky?
While a drip on our outside feels icky.

Wagging their tails is how pretty dog's smile
Girls do the same when testing their guile,
I learned some of this, while in the eighth grade
Whenever Jackie Sugar sashayed!

In the film, Casablanca, Sam played it once more
As Time Goes By was surely the score,
In a popular gin joint often hosting intrigue
Sometimes foiling a German blitzkrieg.

Back to Jackie Sugar, when wearing short skirt
She naturally knew just how to flirt,
When sharpening her pencil in front of the class
She sure wasn't made out of brass.

MAN BITES DOG, the headlines blare
That poor ol' pooch wasn't even aware,
The paper that later picked up his poo
May have protected somebody's shoe.

There once was a gal from Ol' Blighty
Who ran around York in her nightie,
She was so bold, but I was too old
So, I slept all alone in the cold.

Wanna sneak a peek behind Fatima's veil?
Peeping without permission might land you in jail,
But if you are patient and ask very nicely
She might let you glance for a pricely.

The amoeba is single-celled and begets itself
The question is it herself or himself?
It divides itself and does it again
Whenever it's feeling the yen.

There oughta be a shrine to the porcupine
How do two lovers intertwine?
carefully and slowly
Holy guacamole!

The girl next door is hard to ignore.
And looking her way is never a chore,
She's kinda' cute and rarely shy
I'd migrate her way, if she moved to Shanghai.

IF YOU THOUGHT THAT WAS STOOPID, JUST WAIT!

He's Popeye the Sailor Man, toot toot
All decked out in his navy suit, he's cute,
Olive and Wimpy and little Swee'Pee
Waiting at the dock, all footloose and free.

There's so much drama in our good hero's life
But when Bluto's around, there's terrible strife,
All Wimpy wants is hamburger on bun
And even with three, he won't be done.

But around the corner, comes that lowlife villain
He's very able and he's very willin',
Bluto's big and strong and exceedingly ugly
Hate to say it, but he's not a bit snugly.

No worry my friends, 'cause of Popeye's big arms
With spinach in his pocket, sound the alarms,
Some bad words between 'em and a sock on the jaw
Will prove ol' Bluto a houseful of straw, toot toot.

Who do you prefer, Mean Tom or cute Jerry
I betcha they watched them in ol' Tucumcari.
The puss took advantage, at a drop of a hat
Tweety was there with, "I tawt a taw a puddy tat".

"You are my peanut; I am your brittle!"
He wished his loves would be more committal,
He's seeking l'amour, won't take NO, for an answer
Again and again, this skunks an advancer.

Yosemite Sam's an archenemy of Bugs
He yells so much, I sometimes need plugs,
Fourteen Carrot Rabbit and Mutiny on the Bunny
He always gave Sam a run for his money.

No way that Daffy, would be accused of snobbery,
He was kinda funny and his lisp kinda slobbery,
In Yankee Doodle Daffy, the duck is Miranda
Nineteen forty-three fun, with a bit of propaganda.

Bullwinkle J. Moose is a fictional personality
It's hard to believe with his human mentality,
Winkle shares a house with his best friend, Rocky
The two live in Frostbite, where
they play games of hockey.

Well-meaning, dim-witted, and bourgeois
Awarded an Honorary Mooster's Degray,
Active politically, in the Bull Moose party
A good nature finds him, hale and quite hearty.

Remember Marvin the Martian,
in the Haredevil Hare?
Bugs' sent into space, without a wing and a prayer,
Only because of carrots, he's launched to the moon
Came down on the satellite like a leadly balloon.

Mighty Mouse's superpowers include strength and flight
If there is evil in the land, he's ready to fight,
Pretty Pearl Pureheart's his damsel in distress
Defeated the bad guys and earned his success.

OGDEN GNASH WANABEES

· · · · · · · · · ·

Go to Delhi for your belly
If you grave curry in a hurry.

Big Ben goes Tic Tock
A Timex goes tick tock.

Persimmon is a fruit that makes your mouth pucker
Fried, boiled, or braised it's a favorite of Miss Smucker.

Step on a crack you'll break your mother's back
Step on some gum, now that's really dumb,
Tread on protoplasm left by a poodle
Walk carefully home and change your caboodle.

If you have a nosey neighbor who lives next door
Buy a herd of roosters, he'll soon be a bore.

A book by any name is still a book
A girl by any name is worth a second look.

The Isle of Borneo hosts the proud proboscis monkey
The girls of his tribe all consider him hunky,
Deep in South America there dwells a black howler
Really bad news if you're a secretive prowler.

You'll learn a lot if you peruse Jimmy Michener
Might even read about that ol' General Kitchener,

But a study of Churchill or Mr. Mark Twain
Consider it a privilege and a treat for your brain.

If you drive a Ford or even a Chevy
Don't be surprised at a government levy,
If you ride the streetcar or own a horse
You'll be charged less taxes, of course.

The Post Office at Christmas has a really long line
Bring lunch in a sack and hang while you dine,
If you're looking for a short wait
Try church at eight.

Have you ever wondered why the sky is blue?
While right in front of you, there is no hue.

There's a PC ban
On ol' Charlie Chan.

Henry number eight never ran out of wives
The same old gal might have given him hives,
Anne, his second spouse, birthed her Liz
Good Queen Bess ruled like a whiz.

Do the Hoochie Coochie
And your date might get smoochy.

Speaking of snakes, how does a him find a hisss?

I once had a canary whose name was Harry
I got him a partner and named her Sherry.

The good folks who roam the streets around Durban
Drape themselves in saris and turban,
When it's time for supper, one better hurry
Or you might lose out, on a turmerical curry.

If we were the pet and the dog was the master
And if we weren't housebroken, it could cause a disaster,
Go fetch, sit up, lie down, roll over
Would our name be Spot or Fido or Rover?

Thiruvananthapuram boasts both temples and mosques
Up in the minarets, there's spiders and wasps,
Muslims and Hindus along with the Jains,
The clothes they wear do well when it rains.

If candy is dandy and liquor is quicker
How long will it take if you grumble and bicker?

London can be foggy, and Jaipur's kinda hot
Pick a pocket in Hong Kong you're gonna get caught,

Go spend some time in busy Manila
There once were two boxers who put on a thrilla.

Yvonne Lime lived on Lemon Street and
had a Citrus prefix for phone.
A pretty Glendale girl, I placed on a throne.

I wonder what happened to sweet Barbara Ann.
She went to Balboa to get a nice tan.

You must remember your second-grade teacher
She was mentor and nurse and sometimes a preacher.

The Portuguese say Lisboa, and we use Lisbon
Whenever we visit by pedal or piston.

What's the difference between a buzzard and vulture?
Both would know, after all it's their culture.

One doesn't say Aloha
In Krakatoa.

There once was a couple, who moved to Brazil
Before graduation they lived in Seville,
One was named Jack the other was Jill
They sure had trouble navigating that hill.

Faint heart never won a fair maiden
Either brand new or a trade-in.

Have you ever had a pizza
in ol' Chichen Itza?

Pinch a goodie in the kitchen, God forbid
Moms always hear the cookie jar lid.

China has that Imperial Wall
And India's proud of her Taj Mahal,
Paris boasts the Eiffel Tower
While the Dutch brag up their tulip flower.

Londoners hear their loud Big Ben
Kolkata secrets her opium den,
Travelers in Rome behold Coliseum
And Russia's Red Square features a deep mausoleum.

Cairo maintains Pyramids and Sphinx
Edinburgh supports her spacious golf links,
Cape Town is fabulous for old Table Mountain
And Yellowstone's Old Faithful is an on-time fountain.

Munchen has plenty of halls with beir
And Guayaquil's señoritas have no peer.
The Scots claim Haggis, a pudding that's savory
Sheep's heart and lung doesn't seem very flavory.

Hamburger is ground round
Mud pies are round ground.

I remember Shirley Temple
And am friends with Bob Church
But I've never met a Malika Mosque.

If the Redcoats had won,
We'd be saying "Righto",
Instead of "Right on".

In classical ballet, they dance on their toes
Maybe taller prancers might relieve them of woes.

And that ought to settle your hash,
Mister Nash.

YES, IT IS GREEN CHEESE
. . . .

When asked by his sons, "What are
those objects so bright?"
San father thought in the pale winter's night,
"They're the camps where our
grandparents go when they die
They haven't left us, there's no need to cry."

Both Greeks and Mayans oft queried the mysteries
All written down, can be read in their histories,
Copernicus proposed the Geocentric Theory
One century later, the scholars were leery.

Astronomer Galileo with his telescope clear
Examined the cosmos with considerable fear,
Science at odds with a blinkered religion
Pope Paul had forbidden, not even a smidgen

As Dark Ages were ending, there's more to seek
Hopefully, an end to the bleak and the meek,
Ptolemy and Kepler and then later Carl Sagan
With a completely closed mind, it can seem even pagan.

Jules Verne took the folks on a trip to the Moon
Much more than an orb to sit under and spoon,
Now airplanes and rockets were opening the mind
Imagination was rampant for the adventurous kind.

The Cold War was raging, the Soviets 'flew' first
Yanks disappointed, "This must be reversed!"
NASA was prompted by President Kennedy
Find a way to focus, catch up, and remedy.

Apollo placed Armstrong smack on the Moon
American's are proud, a patriot's boon,
As long as humanity looks to the stars
Rockets will be launched to investigate Mars.

Fly me to the Moon
Let me play among the stars
Let me see what Spring is like
On a-Jupiter or Mars

Frank Sinatra

THE BETTER HALF

Jane was the first wife, I shared a trip
Lebanon and Syria were surely a pip,
The Berlin Wall and the Warsaw ballet
We walked the gardens of artist, Monet.

Maria was the second to take a chance
Toured the Holy Land and all that expanse,
The wilds of Africa, then her sis in Durban
After the bushland, it all seemed so urban.

Joanne is third to join expedition
Another blonde, not a real big transition,
In Europe she drove me 7,000 miles
Again, in Africa, where we shared some smiles.

Maggie is the fourth, to join the crusade
Delhi and Agra were on our parade,
Gurus and swamis and Krishna mystics
Tried to master some Yogi linguistics.

Marj and I, then drove the Southwest
Trip went smoothly, you could have guessed,
From the Tularosa Basin to a Pie Town venue
What's your hypothesis on what's on the menu?

YEAHHHHHHH BUDDY

Meet Michael Sweeney, our pal from The Ranch
Took a different turn from humanoid's branch.

Mathematics or football or baseball or beer
Didn't take him long, dispensing some cheer.

It must have been fun to play on his teams
And winning the contest was one of his themes.

Back some years, he took summer weeks
Across the Mississippi and around a few peaks.

Sween attended those games in those parks
Munched many a hotdog with plenty of larks.

It was a VW van in which he would drive
The more he experienced, the more he would thrive.

Chatting it up in the stands, with some of the fans
Gave him an idea, started thinking out plans.

Because baseball was great, football was next
As a ballplayer himself, he needed no text.

Around the country, he drove to each field
And all the exposure those encounters would yield.

Then, six thousand miles on that ol' Russian train
Clickety-clacking Siberian domain.

Mazatlán was maybe his favorite haunt
A spring break holiday, a thousand-mile jaunt.

"A personal friend of the Sween", we proudly claim
Michael's a heck of a lot more than a license plate name.

We said our farewells that day in the gym
The place was filled, right up to the brim.

A List of his buddies would fill up the sheets
And all of his yarns will be told on the streets.

GOTTA KNOW THE TERRITORY
· · · · · · · · ·

ACT ONE

Clickity-clack by rail, travelling salesman complains:
"Rouge vendor's out there, causing honest men pains",
Conductor announces: "NEXT STOP, RIVER CITY"
Only Ioway, but it looks kinda pretty.

"Uses name, Professor Howard Hill
Sells those music fandangles, then collecting on bill,
Doesn't know a lick about music,
leaves towns in the lurch
No scruples at all, would sell whisky to church."

Coach growls to a halt, and a salesman steps out
Looking quite spiffy, but surely no Scout,
There's his name, smack dab on his case
And a confident smirk, smack dab on his face.

'Iowa Stubborn', Harold Hill's next dare
Professor must charm 'em, right there in their lair,
And there's Marcellus, from the good ol' day
Explaining contrariness is River City's way.

Town square's preparing for the Fourth of July
Opportunity to become an uncommon ally,
Rapid-fire sermon 'bout the dangers of pool
"Trouble in River City, pool's the devil's own tool!"

Miss Marion Paroo is the conscience of town
One to convince, if he's gonna stick around
Following her home to continue his con
Brushing off his advances, with a rude, prudish yawn.

Inside school gym, mayor bosses the crowd
Professor attends, declines to be cowed,
"There's trouble in River City, can be solved with a band
Assemble a group, they'll be the best in the land."

"Here on this dotted line, just sign your name
Children's harmonics for pride and for fame,
Mayor again orders his constables four
"Get his credentials, before leaving the door."

Eluding authorities every time after time
Suggesting some songs, sweet harmony's rhyme,
Harold lacks a degree, with zilch to show
If ever they catch him, they'll never be dough.

Follows Marion the Librarian to plead his case
Spinster's a tough sell, but he's enjoying the chase,
Suspicious as heck as Iowan's are
She's appointed herself the 'Cynical Czar'.

Widow Paroo he charms, with the same 'ol tack
Small talk with blarney, he's got the knack,
Troubled young Winthrop, he's lost his dad
He cannot understand and leaving boy sad.

Hill Brags with lie, graduation from Gary
Widow's looking for a man, that Marion can marry,
Winthrop's fired up, may join the group
Be good for the kid to be back in the loop.

Mayor insists, Marion must find College book
Without graduation class, she'll have a long look,
Marion's warming to Harold, he's good for the kid
Taking Winthrop away, from his unhappy skid.

ACT TWO

Flutes, and strings, and gongs, and bells
And horns and drums arrive by Wells
Village excited, they're back to the gym
Now exhibition, it's all up to him.

Bad-tempered salesman, the guy from the train
He's ready to deliver the professor some pain,
His pal from before, just warns him in time
About to inform the town of his crime.

Harold's exposed, it's the end of the line
Tar with feathers, not feeling so fine,
Marion insists, "Let's hear Harold's side first"
If he cannot deliver, his bubble will burst.

Peddler's on the hot spot, hasn't tutored that much
Using phony 'Think System' to teach in the clutch,
Harold Hill's astonished, they almost make tune
And so surprised, he's close to a swoon.

*River City goes nutso, so proud of their band
Professor's relieved and life will be grand,
Surprisingly, kinda playing that Minuet C
A very close call, drama's finished with glee.*

RETURNING FROM SHILOH

The old sergeant was limpin' through town, just lookin'
On his left side there was this long hitchin' post,
Wondered why it caught his eye
Didn't have no horse to tie.

His leg was achin', he knew it always would
And he also knew that others had had it worse,
Some scenes of conflict had left a lastin' scar
The hills beyond, he hoped, would ease that ache afar.

Smithborough was just mostly old honky-tonks
Was a beat-up hotel down a ways, one mile or more,
The drips were falling softly, the
streets mucked from rain
Slowed down his shuffle, a bit more of a strain.

The fella he howdied seemed a cranky ol' bore
Waitin' out this weather must be one nasty chore,
Maybe he would put his head down, up the ways a way
Reckon maybe the corral, out and further on.

Passin' the sheriff's office, they shared the eye
Didn't seem to bother neither one,
A mangey 'ol crow or maybe a raven
Looked things over, reckon it didn't
look like much of a haven.

Then the clouds emptied their burdens once more
And the old timer started thinking again.
Don't need to stop, don't want no job
What he wanted was to get away to the hills.

Was a woman once but she was gone now, but not far
Always up there somewhere inside his head,
Only a bother to him, only now and again
Most times 'round his fire, alone in the night.

At the end of that street of saloons and a mile or so more
Couldn't barely hear them pianos playin' their rag,
The sign to the left was to the hills, and what
was left of the day was mostly gone
Tom hitched in his belt, "Got more walkin'
to do before I see the dawn."

MARY

Whenever Mary walked the lanes, she walked alone
Her beau she lost so many years ago,
To the war, like so many men were lost before
It was the cross she carried through her day.

She picked a leaf and held it to the sun
Venations balanced with the rivers of her life,
She thought, then tossed it to the breeze
And hurried on.

The meadow was her favorite haunt
It was here she wondered, what might have been,
If the guns of war had not taken her Bill away
Such little solace at the end of day.

She sighed and thought, the morrow
might bring some change
But Mary knew her heart, she knew what waited,
Hitching her skirt, she walked the lane back home
To sit the night alone.

Mary knew she'd see her Bill again, one day.

SIGNS OF THE TIMES

DRAGONS, GOBBLINS, AND ORCS---OH, MY!

LIONS, TIGERS, AND BEARS---OH, MY!!

BACTERIUM, VIRUS, AND GERMS---OH, MY!!!

It's finally time to finish. Porky Pig said it best
'Bdya, bdya, bdya, bdya, That's all folks'
Hope you had fun; it was always in jest.